GRAPHIC ORGANIZERS
AND OTHER
VISUAL STRATEGIES

ENGAGE THE
BRAIN

MARCIA L. TATE

CORWIN PRESS
Classroom

For information:

Corwin Press
A SAGE Publications Company
2455 Teller Road
Thousand Oaks, California 91320
CorwinPress.com

SAGE Publications, Ltd.
1 Oliver's Yard
55 City Road
London EC1Y 1SP
United Kingdom

SAGE Publications India Pvt. Ltd.
B 1/I 1 Mohan Cooperative
Industrial Area
Mathura Road, New Delhi
India 110 044

SAGE Publications Asia-Pacific Pvt. Ltd.
33 Pekin Street #02-01
Far East Square
Singapore 048763

Printed in the United States of America.

ISBN 978-1-4129-5232-3

This book is printed on acid-free paper.

08 09 10 11 12 10 9 8 7 6 5 4 3 2 1

Executive Editor: Kathleen Hex
Managing Developmental Editor: Christine Hood
Editorial Assistant: Anne O'Dell
Developmental Writer: Q. L. Pearce
Developmental Editor: Karen Hall
Proofreader: Bette Darwin
Art Director: Anthony D. Paular
Cover Designer: Monique Hahn
Interior Production Artist: Scott Van Atta
Illustrator: Robbie Short
Design Consultant: PUMPKiN PIE Design

GRADES **6-8**

SCIENCE

ENGAGE THE BRAIN

TABLE OF CONTENTS

Connections to Standards

This chart shows the national science standards that are covered in each chapter.

SCIENCE AS INQUIRY	Standards are covered on pages
Ability to conduct scientific inquiry.	9, 21, 35, 44, 54, 61, 93
Understand about scientific inquiry.	9, 21, 35, 44, 54, 61, 93

PHYSICAL SCIENCE	Standards are covered on pages
Understand properties and changes of properties in matter.	12, 15, 18, 21, 24, 31, 35
Understand motions and forces.	12, 15, 18, 21, 24, 31, 35
Understand transfer of energy.	12, 15, 18, 21, 24, 31, 35

LIFE SCIENCE	Standards are covered on pages
Understand structure and function in living systems.	38, 41, 44, 47, 51, 54, 57, 61, 64
Understand reproduction and heredity.	38, 41, 44, 47, 51, 54, 57, 61, 64
Understand regulation and behavior.	38, 41, 44, 47, 51, 54, 57, 61, 64
Understand populations and ecosystems.	38, 41, 44, 47, 51, 54, 57, 61, 64
Understand diversity and adaptations of organisms.	38, 41, 44, 47, 51, 54, 57, 61, 64

EARTH AND SPACE SCIENCE	Standards are covered on pages
Understand structure of the earth system.	67, 70, 74, 77, 81, 84, 87, 90, 93
Understand Earth's history.	67, 70, 74, 77, 81, 84, 87, 90, 93
Understand Earth in the solar system.	67, 70, 74, 77, 81, 84, 87, 90, 93

Introduction

An ancient Chinese proverb claims: "Tell me, I forget. Show me, I remember. Involve me, I understand." This timeless saying insinuates what all educators should know: Unless students are involved and actively engaged in learning, true learning rarely occurs.

The latest brain research reveals that both the right and left hemispheres of the brain should be engaged in the learning process. This is important because the hemispheres talk to one another over the corpus callosum, the structure that connects them. No strategies are better designed for this purpose than graphic organizers and visuals. Both of these strategies engage students' visual modality. More information goes into the brain visually than through any other modality. Therefore, it makes sense to take advantage of students' visual strengths to reinforce and make sense of learning.

How to Use This Book

Correlated with the national standards for science, the activities in this book are designed using strategies that actively engage the brain. They are presented in the way the brain learns best, to make sure students get the most out of each lesson: focus activity, modeling, guided practice, check for understanding, independent practice, and closing. Go through each step to ensure that students will be fully engaged in the concept being taught and understand its purpose and meaning.

Each step-by-step activity provides one or more visual tools students can use to make important connections between related concepts, structure their thinking, organize ideas logically, and reinforce learning. Graphic organizers and visuals include: network tree, word map, props, project planner, sensory chart, word wall, bar graph, cause-and-effect map, trading cards, models, comparison chart, cycle chart, posters, puzzles, timelines, pie chart, triple Venn diagram, and more!

These brain-compatible activities are sure to engage and motivate every student's brain in your classroom! Watch your students change from passive to active learners as they process visual concepts into learning that is not only fun, but remembered for a lifetime.

Put It Into Practice

Lecture and repetitive worksheets have long been the traditional way of delivering knowledge and reinforcing learning. While some higher-achieving students may engage in this type of learning, educators now know that actively engaging students' brains is not a luxury, but a necessity if students are truly to acquire and retain content, not only for tests, but for life.

The 1990s were dubbed the Decade of the Brain because millions of dollars were spent on brain research. Educators today should know more about how students learn than ever before. Learning style theories that call for student engagement have been proposed for decades, as evidenced by research such as Howard Gardner's theory of multiple intelligences (1983), Bernice McCarthy's 4MAT Model (1990), and VAKT (visual, auditory, kinesthetic, tactile) learning styles theories.

I have identified 20 strategies that, according to brain research and learning style theory, appear to correlate with the way the brain learns best. I have observed hundreds of teachers—regular education, special education, and gifted. Regardless of the classification or grade level of the students, exemplary teachers consistently use these 20 strategies to deliver memorable classroom instruction and help their students understand and retain vast amounts of content.

These 20 brain-based instructional strategies include the following:

1. Brainstorming and Discussion

2. Drawing and Artwork

3. Field Trips

4. Games

5. Graphic Organizers, Semantic Maps, and Word Webs

6. Humor

7. Manipulatives, Experiments, Labs, and Models

8. Metaphors, Analogies, and Similes

9. Mnemonic Devices

10. Movement

11. Music, Rhythm, Rhyme, and Rap

12. Project-based and Problem-based Instruction

13. Reciprocal Teaching and Cooperative Learning

14. Role Plays, Drama, Pantomimes, Charades

15. Storytelling

16. Technology

17. Visualization and Guided Imagery

18. Visuals

19. Work Study and Apprenticeships

20. Writing and Journals

This book features Strategy 5: Graphic Organizers, Semantic Maps, and Word Webs, and Strategy 18: Visuals. Both strategies integrate visual and verbal elements of learning. Picture thinking, visual thinking, and visual/spatial learning is the phenomenon of thinking through visual processing. Since 90% of the brain's sensory input comes from visual sources, it stands to reason that the most powerful influence on learners' behavior is concrete, visual images. (Jensen, 1994) Also, linking verbal and visual images increases students' ability to store and retrieve information. (Ogle, 2000)

Graphic organizers are visual representations of linear ideas that benefit both left and right hemispheres of the brain. They assist us in making sense of information, enable us to search for patterns, and provide an organized tool for making important conceptual connections. Graphic organizers, also known as word webs or semantic, mind, and concept maps, can be used to plan lessons or present information to students. Once familiar with the technique, students should be able to construct their own graphic organizers, reflecting their understanding of the concepts taught.

Because we live in a highly visual world, using visuals as a teaching strategy makes sense. Each day, students are overwhelmed with images from video games, computers, and television. Visual strategies capitalize specifically on the one modality that many students use consistently—the visual modality. Visuals include overheads, maps, graphs, charts, and other concrete objects that clarify learning. Since so much sensory input comes from visual sources, pictures, words, and artifacts around the classroom take on exaggerated importance in students' brains. Visuals such as these provide learning support and constant reinforcement.

These strategies help students make sense of learning by focusing on ways the brain learns best. Fully supported by the latest brain research, these strategies provide the tools you need to boost motivation, energy, and most important, the academic achievement of your students.

CHAPTER 1

Physical Science

Scientific Method: Ladder Graphic Organizer

Skills Objectives
Understand the nature of scientific inquiry.
Use prior knowledge.
Form a hypothesis.
Conduct a scientific investigation.

The Scientific Method is a step-by-step process used to make observations and test a hypothesis. A **Ladder Graphic Organizer** is an excellent visual tool that encourages students to remember each step of the scientific process. It also helps build a bridge between ideas. Using a ladder graphic organizer when designing an experiment will help students to plan before they begin.

1. Begin a discussion about the scientific method by asking volunteers to describe a step-by-step activity such as shooting a basketball or baking a cake. Encourage them to use words such as *then, next,* and *after that.*

2. Write the sentence **P**aul **O**livera **H**ad **E**xtra **C**hange on the board. Explain that the sentence is known as a mnemonic device, a tool to help remember information. The first letter of each word stands for a step in the scientific method: **P**roblem, **O**bservation, **H**ypothesis, **E**xperiment, **C**onclusion.

3. Draw a sample of the **Scientific Method Ladder reproducible (page 11)** on the board or on an overhead transparency. Tell students that they are going to do an experiment to demonstrate the scientific method. They will see if sugar changes when mixed with warm water. Ask: *What is the first step in planning an experiment?* (Identify the problem.) In the space below the bottom rung labeled *Problem*, write: *Will sugar change in warm water?*

4. Guide students through the second step of the scientific method, *Making Observations*. Ask a volunteer to feel the sugar and describe the texture and appearance. Have another volunteer feel and describe the water. Write their comments below the rung labeled *Observations*.

Materials
Scientific Method Ladder reproducible

1/4 cup sugar

1 cup warm water

glass or jar

spoon

5. The third step is *Forming a Hypothesis*. Explain that a hypothesis is an educated guess; you combine what you already know and what you learned from your observations to predict what will happen when you mix the sugar in water. Ask a volunteer to suggest a hypothesis for you to write below the rung labeled *Hypothesis. (The sugar will dissolve.)*

6. Remind students that an experiment should be designed to test the hypothesis, not just to prove that it is correct. Prompt students to think of a procedure for the experiment. For example: *Pour sugar in water. Stir for one minute. Wait five minutes. Check water.* Write the steps in the space below the rung labeled *Experiment.* Then invite volunteers to help you conduct the experiment.

7. Reread the problem in Step 3, and discuss the data gathered from the experiment. Ask a student to suggest a conclusion about the experiment, and write it below the rung labeled *Conclusion. (The sugar dissolved in warm water.)* Ask: *Did the conclusion support the hypothesis or disprove it?* Point out that a conclusion might lead to another question, such as: *Will sugar dissolve in cold water? Will it dissolve faster or slower?*

8. Give students a copy of the Scientific Method Ladder reproducible, and have them design a simple experiment to conduct at home. Make sure students understand how to use the graphic organizer to record each step, and check that their experiments can be done safely with simple materials.

9. After experiments have been completed, allow class time for students to present their results, and display their graphic organizers on a bulletin board.

Extended Learning

Have students use the scientific method and a ladder graphic organizer to design a new experiment based on the one done in class. Have them change one variable, such as adding twice as much sugar, substituting salt for sugar, or substituting ice water for warm water. Have students predict how their results might change in each case. Then have them test their hypothesis at home or in class to see if they are correct.

Scientific Method Ladder

Directions: Review the steps of the scientific method. Then "climb" the ladder by writing each step in the space below each rung.

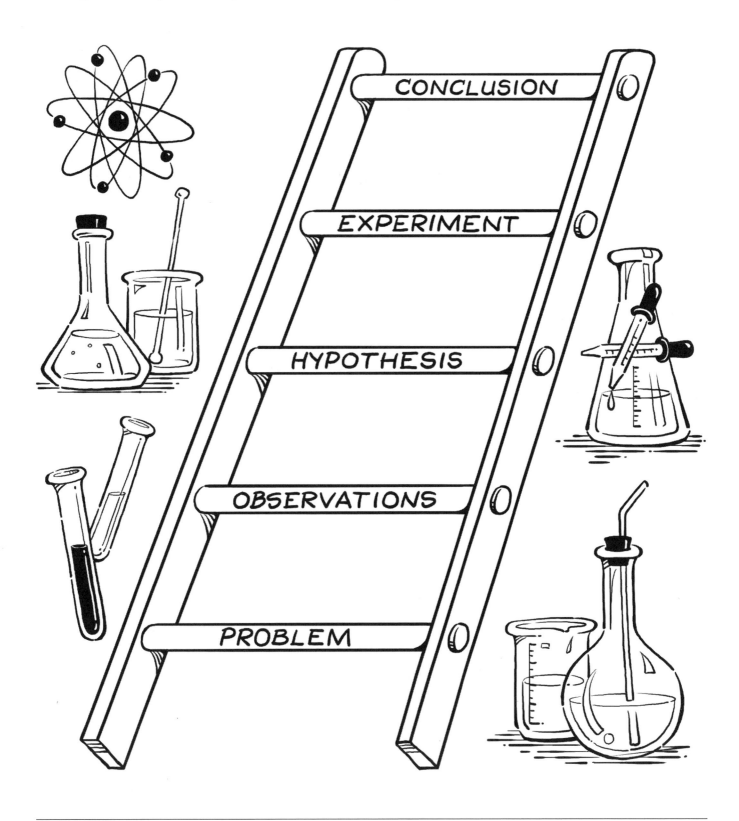

CONCLUSION

EXPERIMENT

HYPOTHESIS

OBSERVATIONS

PROBLEM

Properties of Matter: Bulletin Board

Materials

Properties of Matter reproducible

thin tree branch

sheet of paper

research materials about the properties of matter

Skills Objectives

Understand the difference between physical and chemical properties.
Recognize cause and effect.
Predict outcomes.

The chemical properties of matter are often difficult for students to understand. A demonstration of a physical property is simple, but a demonstration of a chemical property is not always practical in a classroom setting. Creating a **Bulletin Board** display can offer an attractive solution. The bulletin board acts as a "snapshot" that helps students internalize the information shown. It is a safe and effective way to illustrate the difference between physical and chemical properties of matter.

1. Tell students that matter can be described in two ways—by its physical properties and by its chemical properties. Hold up a tree branch, and ask students to describe its physical properties (what they notice with their senses). Pass the branch around the class, and ask students to describe how it looks, feels, and smells. Then break the branch in half. Ask: *How have I changed the branch? Is it still wood?* Point out that although the size is different, it's still wood; its form has been altered, but not its identity.

2. Tell students that all substances of matter have chemical properties that can't always be seen or felt. Ask: *If I burn this branch, will the substance left behind still be wood?* (No; it will be ash.) Explain that combustibility, or the ability to be burned, is a chemical property of wood.

3. Hold up the branch in one hand and a sheet of paper in the other. Point out that they both come from a tree. Ask students: *Would changing this branch into paper involve chemical changes, physical changes, or both?* (both) Explain that chemical changes are permanent; they can't be reversed to their original form.

4. Give students a copy of the **Properties of Matter reproducible (page 14)**. Model using the reproducible by drawing an apple on the board and writing below it: *Physical Properties—red, sweet, round, hard; Chemical Properties—decomposes, turns brown when in contact with oxygen.*

5. Tell students to draw their own object or substance on their reproducible and write below it the physical and chemical properties of that object. Encourage them to think of objects seen

in school, at home, or in their neighborhood. Write the following *Did You Know?* passage on the board for students to use for ideas.

Did You Know?

With our senses, we can detect physical properties such as taste, smell, color, texture, flexibility, luster, hardness, density, thermal expansion, conductivity, electrical resistance, boiling and melting temperature, and solubility.

The chemical properties of a substance describe its potential to react with or change into a new substance. Examples include flammability, decomposition, and oxidation (such as iron that rusts, fruit that turns brown, or metal that tarnishes). Everyday examples of chemical reactions include cooking (caramelized sugar), fermentation (used in winemaking), or the bubbling seen when an antacid tablet is dropped in water. Some clues that a chemical reaction is taking place are color change, production of heat or light, and the formation of a gas.

---

6. Create a bulletin board display of students' work titled *Physical and Chemical Properties of Matter*. Encourage students to add pictures and small objects to the display. Discuss the results and ask questions to confirm that students understand the difference between physical and chemical properties of matter.

Extended Learning

- Have students create a bulletin board display showing objects classified by physical or chemical properties. For example, ask: *What types of things burn? Are flexible? Have a low melting point? Conduct electricity?*

- Tell students physical changes may often be reversed (water can be frozen into ice, melted to a liquid, and heated to water vapor), whereas chemical reactions usually cannot. You can't uncook an egg or un-burn wood. Ask students if it's possible to dissolve sugar in water and reverse the process, and if so, how.

- Introduce students to the Periodic Table of Elements. Explain how placement on the table gives clues to the properties of individual elements and compounds. As you describe the elements in each group or family, ask students whether those characteristics are physical or chemical properties.

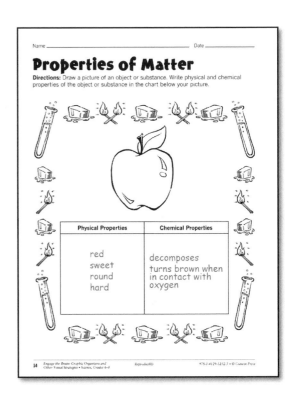

Name _____   Date _____

Properties of Matter

Directions: Draw a picture of an object or substance. Write physical and chemical properties of the object or substance in the chart below your picture.

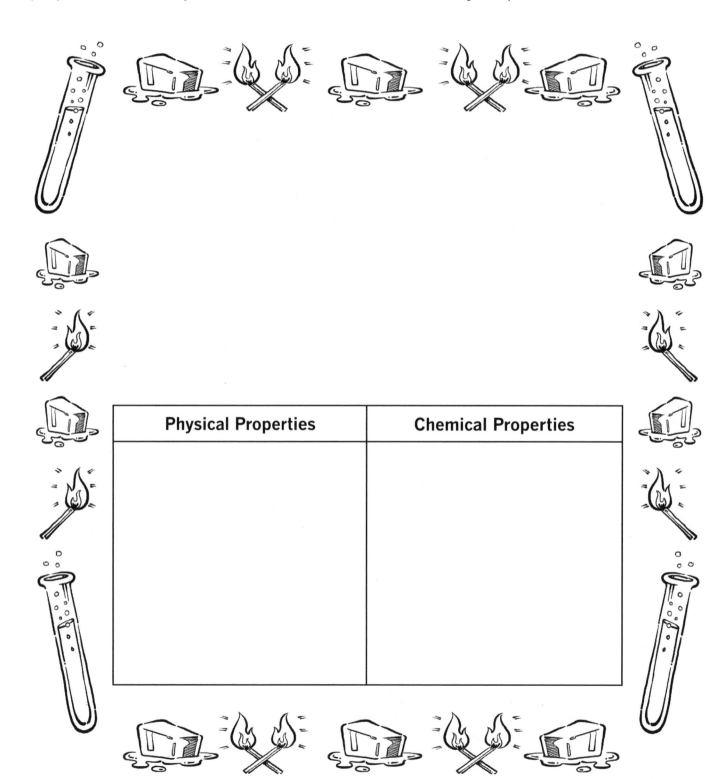

Physical Properties	Chemical Properties

Engage the Brain: Graphic Organizers and
Other Visual Strategies • Science, Grades 6–8   Reproducible   978-1-4129-5232-3 • © Corwin Press

Facts on Film: Media and T-Chart

Skills Objectives
Predict an outcome.
Distinguish between fact and opinion.

Materials
Fact or Opinion
T-Chart reproducible

The wonders of technology can provide an invaluable tool in the classroom. **Media** such as videocassettes, CD-ROMs, DVDs, and the Internet offer many teaching options. Watching a presentation enhances listening skills and appeals to visually oriented learners. As a pre-reading activity, media provide students with a bank of knowledge to apply to class lessons and can help put information in context. As a postreading activity, media can reinforce learning.

1. Select a recorded program about a science topic you're currently teaching. You may check your local library or video store or use a television broadcast. (See suggestions on the following page.) Be sure to preview any program before you decide to show it.

2. Before the class views the program, give students a copy of the **Fact or Opinion T-Chart reproducible (page 17)**. Graphic organizers such as a T-chart can be handy when using media in the classroom. Explain to students that they will be using their T-chart during and after the presentation.

3. Demonstrate how to use the Fact or Opinion T-Chart by drawing a sample on the board or using an overhead. First, ask students to explain the difference between a fact and an opinion. *(A fact is something that is proven to be true; an opinion is a judgment or personal point of view.)* Then ask: *Which of these statements is a fact, and which is an opinion? An apple is a fruit. An apple is the best fruit.* Invite a volunteer to write the statements in the correct column of your chart. Then ask students to suggest other examples of facts and opinions to add to the chart.

4. List on the board some important names and topics from the program you are going to show, and review them with the class. Tell students to listen to the program for at least three facts and three opinions about those names and topics and write the facts and opinions on their T-Chart.

5. Start the presentation, leaving on some lights for students to take notes. Pause at key points and check for comprehension, answer students' questions, point out clues, or have students make predictions.

6. After the viewing, initiate a class discussion about the show. Ask students to share and compare the information they recorded on their Fact or Opinion T-Chart.

Examples of Media for the Science Classroom

Changes in the Properties of Matter
Running Time: 28 minutes
www.schoolvideos.com

Common Properties of Matter: Atoms, Elements, and States
Running Time: 24 minutes
www.schoolvideos.com

Matter: Changes in the Properties of Matter: Physical and Chemical
Running Time: 28 minutes
www.clearvue.com

Internet site about using television in the classroom:
www.pbs.org/teachersource/tvteachers.htm

Extended Learning

- Divide the class into small groups to discuss the media selection. Have them write a review summarizing and illustrating their thoughts.

- Choose a follow-up activity, such as an experiment or field trip, that will connect the presentation to a real-life experience.

- Ask students to recommend television shows or films that might enhance the unit you are studying.

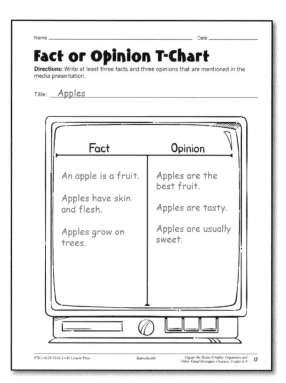

Name _____ Date _____

Fact or Opinion T-Chart

Directions: Write at least three facts and three opinions that are mentioned in the media presentation.

Title: _____

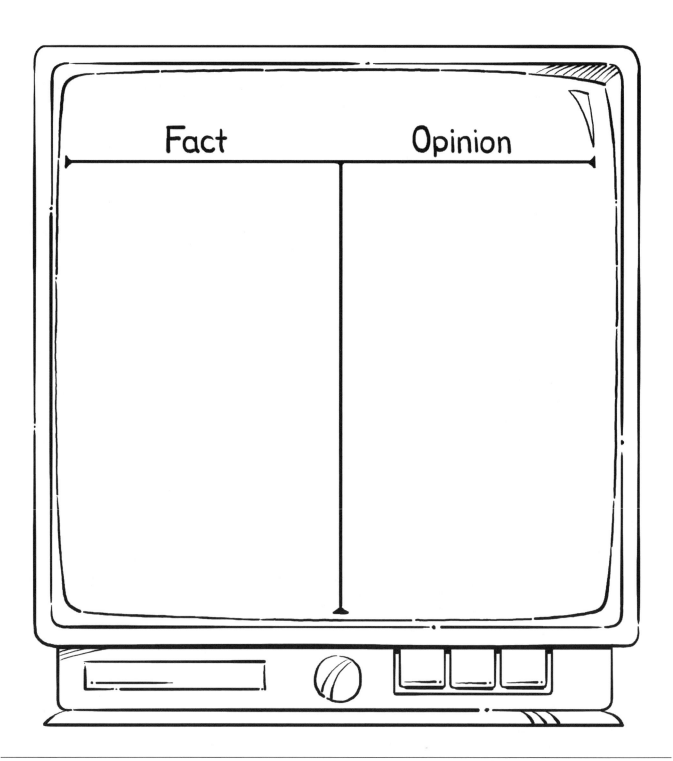

Fact	Opinion

Science Vocabulary: Word Map

Skills Objectives

Use prior knowledge to find word meaning.

Use dictionary skills.

Use word association to enhance learning.

In science, students must be able to communicate ideas. An expansive vocabulary is critical to communicating those ideas effectively. A **Word Map** is a graphic organizer that helps students build their vocabulary. Rather than just memorize words and terms, students can use the map to help them retain learning, use vocabulary in context, and develop a framework on which to build new knowledge. A word map also works well as a prereading or postreading activity.

1. Vocabulary words are often remembered because of meaningful associations rather than repetition. To demonstrate how a word clue or association can be used, tell students that the prefix *tele-* means "at a distance" and is used to describe instruments that operate over distance. Prompt students to list words that begin with the prefix *tele-*, such as *telephone, television, telegraph,* and *telephoto.* Write the words on the board. Discuss how knowing the meaning of the prefix *tele-* offers a clue about the meaning of the word.

2. Draw a simple word map on the board, and give students a copy of the **Vocabulary Word Map reproducible (page 20)**. Distribute dictionaries, and write the following vocabulary list on the board (or use your own list): *combustibility, malleability, conductivity, insulator, mixture, solution, solubility.*

3. Demonstrate how to fill in the Vocabulary Word Map. Write *combustibility* in the center circle. Ask a volunteer to use prior knowledge to guess the word's meaning. Write the answer in the box labeled *My Definition.*

4. Then have students look up the definition of *combustibility* in a dictionary. Have them tell you what to write in the box labeled *Dictionary Definition.*

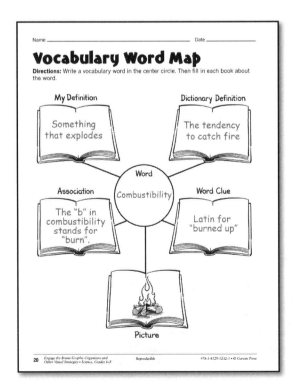

5. Point out that a dictionary often includes the origin of the word or root word. Knowing the origin of a word can help students remember the definition. For *combustibility*, the origin of its root word *combust* means "burned up." Write the word origin or other clues in the box labeled *Word Clue*.

6. Have students suggest a picture that shows the meaning of the word. Draw one of their suggestions, such as a match or campfire, in the box labeled *Picture*.

7. The last box labeled *Association* is for any clue that will help a student remember the definition of the word. For example: *The **b** in combustibility stands for **b**urn*. Have students brainstorm several possible associations, and write one of their suggestions in the box. Review the completed map with students, and check for understanding.

8. Invite students to complete their own vocabulary word map using another word from the vocabulary list. After they finish, have students with the same vocabulary word compare their results.

9. Invite students to read their vocabulary word maps to the class. Discuss how word clues can help them remember vocabulary words.

Extended Learning

- Encourage students to complete word maps for new science vocabulary taught throughout the year. They can store the maps in a binder or a science portfolio.

- Use pairs of index cards to create vocabulary sets, one card with the vocabulary word and one card with the definition. Give half of the class vocabulary cards and the other half definition cards. Have students take turns asking questions to find their vocabulary word or definition match.

- Use a variety of word searches, crosswords, scrambled words, and other kinds of word puzzles to help students learn science vocabulary. You may go online to find resources, such as Jefferson Lab at: *http://education.jlab.org/vocabhangman*.

Name _____   Date _____

Vocabulary Word Map

Directions: Write a vocabulary word in the center circle. Then fill in each book about the word.

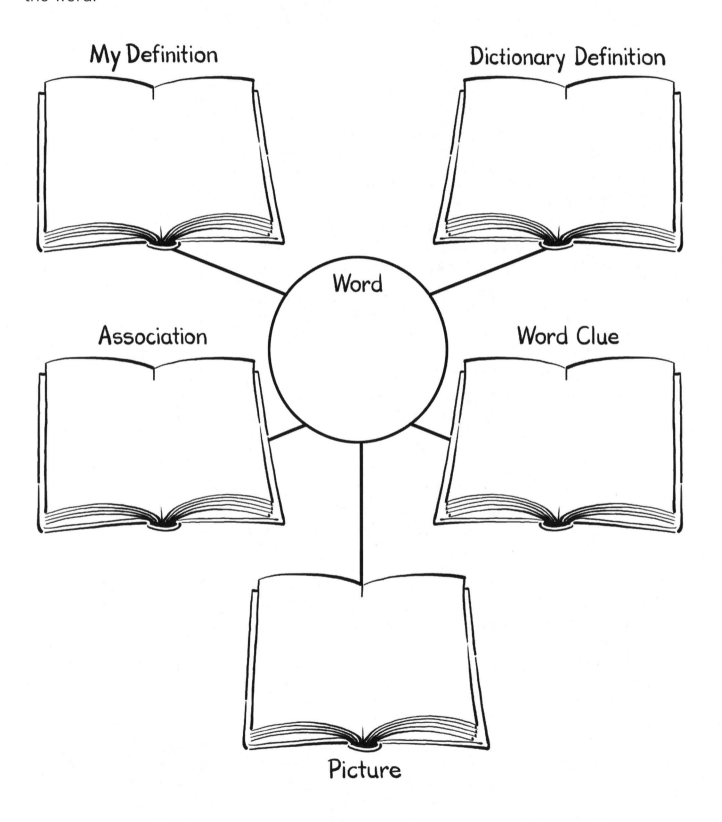

My Definition

Dictionary Definition

Word

Association

Word Clue

Picture

*Engage the Brain: Graphic Organizers and
Other Visual Strategies • Science, Grades 6–8*   *Reproducible*   978-1-4129-5232-3 • © Corwin Press

Tools of the Trade: Props and Line Graph

Skills Objectives
Use appropriate tools to collect data.
Use graphs to analyze data.

Materials
Graph It! reproducible

balance scales

small objects (weighing one pound or less)

Through the use of tools such as **Props** in inquiry-based learning, students gain knowledge from their own experiences. Most students respond well to hands-on activities that include the use of standard science tools, such as balance scales, thermometers, and microscopes. Providing your class with the opportunity to use such tools, along with a **Line Graph**, helps them achieve a better understanding of science concepts and increases their retention of key points.

1. Introduce students to the idea of using tools by initiating a discussion about common, everyday tools. Ask: *What tool do you use when you write something?* Point out that a pencil or pen is a writing tool. Ask students to suggest other simple tools found in the classroom or at home (e.g., *balance scale, magnifying glass, thermometer, ruler, meter stick, calculator, hammer, screwdriver*).

2. Tell students that they will use a common tool to measure the force of gravity on small objects and will record those measurements on a line graph. Ask students to define the word *force* (*an influence that acts upon a body to change its motion or produce stress*). Explain that a *scale* is a tool that measures the force of gravity on an object, or the weight of that object. On Earth, gravity is the attractive force that pulls objects toward Earth's center. The weight of an object is a measurement of gravitational force on the object; the amount of gravitational force depends on the mass of the object (the amount of matter in it).

3. Give students a copy of the **Graph It! reproducible (page 23)**, and draw a copy on the board or use an overhead to guide the class. Help students decide what increments to use for the number scale (either ounces or grams, depending on your balance scale). Point out that all the objects weigh less than one pound. (Remind them that one pound equals 16 ounces; two pounds is about one kilogram; and one kilogram equals 1,000 grams.)

4. Demonstrate how to use the scale by weighing an object as the class observes. Encourage students to predict the weight of the object before you weigh it. Then show students how to plot and

label the actual weight on the graph, while students do the same on their paper. Repeat the process with two more objects, inviting volunteers to help weigh and record the measurements. Show how to connect the dots to form a line graph.

5. Once you are certain that students understand how to use the scale and plot their results on the graph, divide the class into groups of three or four. Have groups take turns weighing and recording seven more objects of their choice for a total of ten.

6. When all the graphs are complete, invite students to share what they learned, answering questions such as: *Which object was the lightest? The heaviest? What was the most common weight? What is the average weight of all the objects?* Encourage students to think of additional questions based on their own experiences using the scale.

Extended Learning

- Have more advanced students convert their measurements to *newtons* (the SI unit of weight) and graph those values instead: *Weight (N) = Mass (kg) x Acceleration due to gravity (9.8 m/s2).*

- Have students suggest other types of graphs used to display data (e.g., *bar graph, pie chart*) and graph their results using one of those methods.

- Remind students that weight is determined by gravitational force, which varies throughout the universe, whereas mass is always constant. Encourage students to go to the Exploratorium® Web site at *www.exploratorium.edu/ronh/weight* and discover how much they and their objects would weigh on different planets or moons.

- Discuss other forces, such as magnetic force and frictional force. Ask students: *What tools would be best to measure those forces?* Divide the class into small groups, and have each group design a way to use a tool to measure each force.

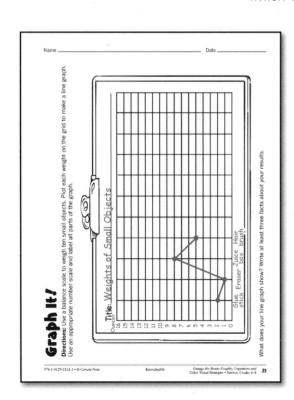

Graph It!

Directions: Use a balance scale to weigh ten small objects. Plot each weight on the grid to make a line graph. Use an appropriate number scale and label all parts of the graph.

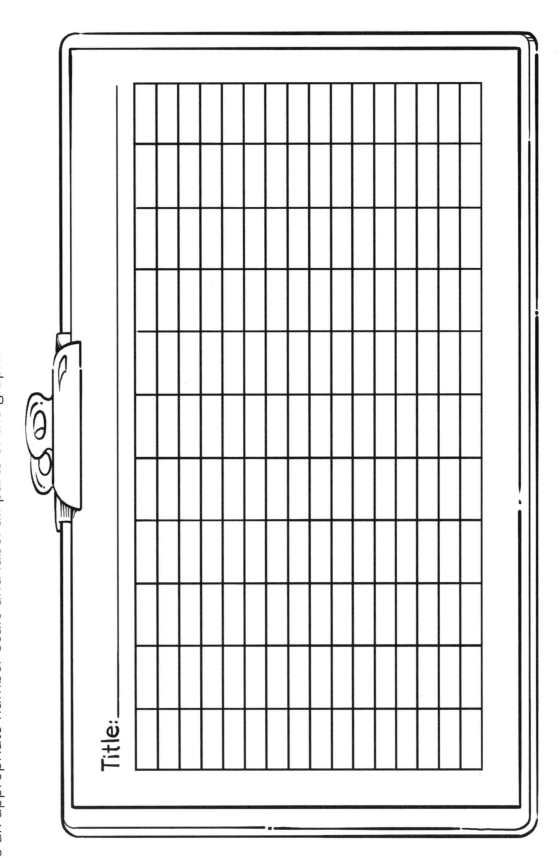

Title: _____

What does your line graph show? Write at least three facts about your results.

Force and Motion: Chain of Events Map

Materials

Chain of Events Map reproducible

baseball

Skills Objectives

Recognize cause-and-effect relationships.

Understand sequence.

Predict a result.

A **Chain of Events Map** is a tool that allows students to show information in steps or stages. It can help students describe a sequence of events, such as the result of application of force or forces over a period of time. This organizer guides students to visualize how one action or event leads to another and ultimately to a logical outcome. By mapping a chain of events, students can more easily see how everyday occurrences are linked to the forces at work around us.

1. Draw a copy of the **Chain of Events Map reproducible (page 26)** on the board, or reproduce it on an overhead transparency. Explain to students that a chain of events map can help them show a sequence of events. To demonstrate, gently toss a baseball into the air, and let it fall to the floor. Ask: *What caused the ball to come down?* (gravity, air resistance) *What was the chain of events for the ball?*

2. Write the sequence of events in the organizer from start to finish. *(I tossed the ball. Gravity and air resistance acted on it. The ball stopped going up. The ball fell down. The ball hit the floor.)*

3. Map out another chain of events, this time for a bicycle. Ask students to name a force that affects the motion of a bicycle. *(gravity, friction)* Then ask: *What starts the sequence of events? Does the rider begin the action by applying a downward force to the pedal? What happens next? Do the wheels of the bicycle begin to rotate? Does the bicycle move forward?* Go through the activity step by step, ending with the final step of applying the brakes to stop the bicycle.

4. Give students a copy of the Chain of Events Map reproducible to complete on their own or with a partner. Tell students they may use any sequence of events that shows the interaction between force and motion. Help students brainstorm ideas, prompting them to think of moving objects at home or in their neighborhood.

5. As they work, make sure students understand that each event must lead directly to the next event. Encourage students to refer to the class example on display.

6. When they're finished, invite students to present their maps to the class, stopping just before the last event. Allow the class to guess the final outcome.

Extended Learning

- Ask students to bring in newspaper articles that show a chain of events in nature, such as strong winds causing a tree to fall onto a car or flooding causing a structure to wash away. Lead the class in identifying each sequence of events mentioned in the articles.

- Have students predict the outcome of an unexpected force acting on an object. For example, ask: *What would happen if a skateboarder riding down a smooth sidewalk suddenly hit a patch of sand? What forces would be at work?*

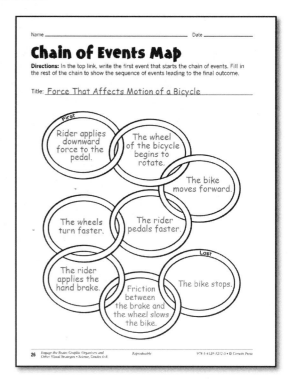

Name _____ Date _____

Chain of Events Map

Directions: In the top link, write the first event that starts the chain of events. Fill in the rest of the chain to show the sequence of events leading to the final outcome.

Title: _____

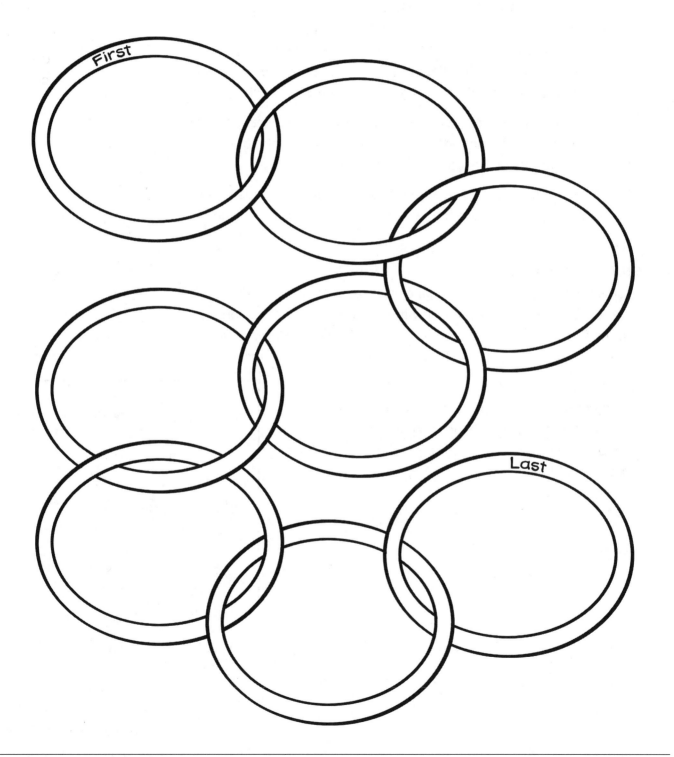

Laws of Motion: Main Idea and Details Chart

Skills Objectives
Read for a purpose.
Use prior knowledge.
Identify main idea and supporting details.

Materials

Measuring Motion reproducible

Main Idea and Details Chart reproducible

overhead projector and transparency

A **Main Idea and Details Chart** helps students to think actively while reading text. Once completed, the chart gives students an at-a-glance reference for a topic, main ideas, and supporting details. This organizer can be used to gather background information for an essay or report or as a study guide for exams.

1. To help students understand the meaning of *main idea,* whisper a topic to a student, and have him or her say a few words or clues about that topic. For example, the student could list soccer equipment for the topic of *soccer.* Then ask students: *What was the main idea for these clues or details?* Have students cite one or two details to support their answer.

2. Give students a copy of the **Measuring Motion** and **Main Idea and Details Chart reproducibles (pages 29–30)**. Tell the class they will be using the chart to summarize the main ideas and supporting details of the article "Measuring Motion." Remind students that the main idea is the central thought or most important idea of the article. Ask: *Why do you think there are three Main Idea sections on this chart?* Point out that there are three paragraphs in the article and that each has its own main idea.

3. Ask a couple of volunteers to read aloud "Measuring Motion" as the rest of the class listens. Then place a transparency of the Main Idea and Details Chart reproducible on the overhead projector. Ask students: *What is the topic of this article?* Write *Motion* in the box labeled *Topic.*

4. Ask students to reread the first paragraph silently to find the main idea. Explain that some paragraphs specifically state the main idea as a summary sentence, whereas other paragraphs have an

implied main idea based on key facts in the paragraph. Ask: *Is the main idea of the first paragraph stated or implied?* (implied) *What is the main idea?* (defining motion) Repeat the process for the second and third paragraphs. *(speed, velocity)*

5. Once main ideas are recorded, encourage students to suggest details to write in the boxes below the main ideas. For example: *Motion—any change in position; Speed—how far and how long in motion; Velocity—can change without changing speed.*

6. After completing the sample chart, divide the class into small groups. Assign each group a reading passage from your science textbook, and have them complete their Main Idea and Details Chart about it. Check students' progress as they work to make sure they understand how to complete each part of the chart.

7. Have each group share their finished charts. Ask students: *What was the main idea of each paragraph? What clues helped you figure out the main idea? What was the main idea of the entire passage?* Point out that the main idea of the entire passage should encompass the main ideas of all the paragraphs.

Extended Learning

- Provide students with old newspapers and magazines, and have them complete a Main Idea and Details Chart about an article of their choosing. Encourage them to highlight or underline key facts in the text as they read their article.

- Ask students to work together to create a Laws of Motion poster based on the format of the Main Idea and Details Chart.

- Have students use a Main Idea and Details Chart for review before a test. For example, they can work in groups to review a chapter in their textbook, fill out a chart together, and make copies of the chart to take home for studying.

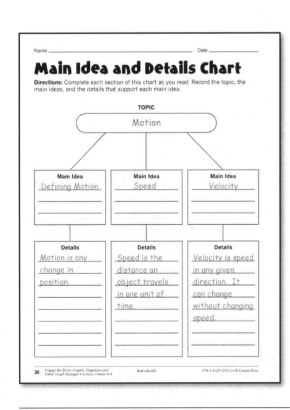

Measuring Motion

Motion is any change in the position of an object. Things move when they are pushed or pulled by a force or caused to fall by **gravity**. You could have the fastest skateboard in the neighborhood, but it wouldn't move an inch unless you were pushed or got on and pushed against the ground with one foot.

One way to measure motion is to figure out how fast the object is going. That is its **speed**. To calculate speed, you need to know the distance the object travels in one unit of time. For example, if you rode your skateboard five miles in one hour, your speed would be five miles per hour.

Velocity is another measurement of motion. To calculate velocity, you need to know the distance the object travels in one unit of time as well as the direction the object is traveling. In other words, velocity is the speed in a given direction. You can change velocity without changing speed. For example, let's say you are riding your skateboard at five miles per hour in a northward direction. If you make a left turn without slowing down at all, your speed won't change but your velocity will. Your velocity will be five miles per hour westward.

For a spacecraft, **escape velocity** is the minimum speed needed to escape the gravitational pull of a planet. Escape velocity from Earth's surface is about seven miles per second.

Name _____ Date _____

Main Idea and Details Chart

Directions: Complete each section of this chart as you read. Record the topic, the main ideas, and the details that support each main idea.

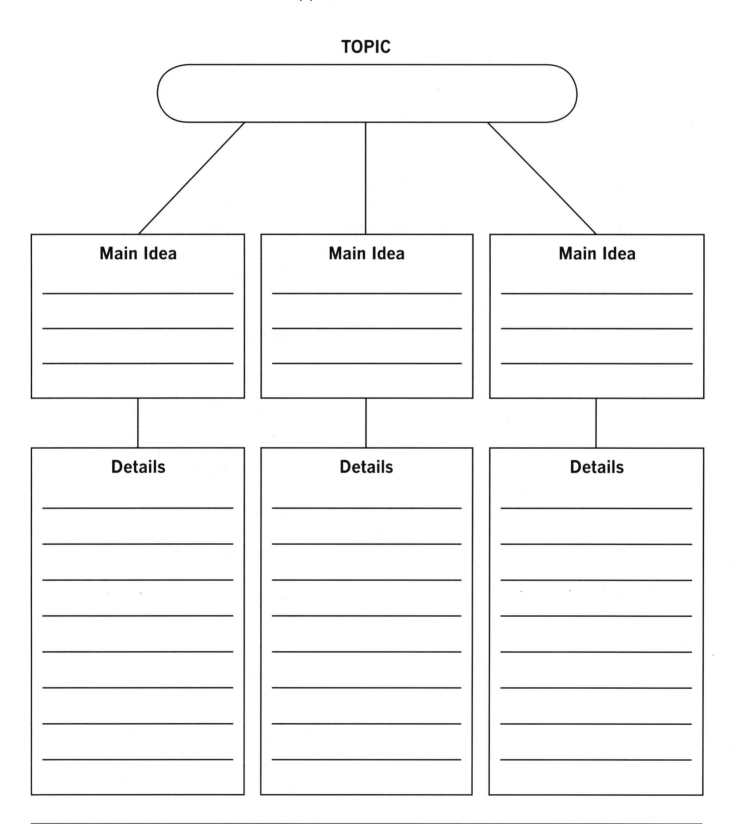

TOPIC

Main Idea	Main Idea	Main Idea

Details	Details	Details

Engage the Brain: Graphic Organizers and Other Visual Strategies • Science, Grades 6–8   Reproducible   978-1-4129-5232-3 • © Corwin Press

Lots of Energy: Network Tree Organizer

Skills Objectives
Use prior knowledge.
Understand hierarchal reasoning.
Evaluate and organize data sets.

Materials
Lots of Energy reproducible

Network Tree Organizer reproducible

science resources about energy

overhead projector and transparency

A **Network Tree Organizer** is a hierarchical graphic organizer that can be used to sort and classify scientific information and show how different parts are related. Using this organizer is an excellent way for students to get a clear overview of otherwise complex topics and to organize data from multiple sources and reflect superordinate or subordinate elements.

1. To help students understand how a network tree organizer works, write the topic *clothing* on the board, and ask students to list different categories of clothing for you to write in a row below it. For example, you could write *shirts, hats, shoes, pants*, and *coats*. Then ask students to suggest two specific items to write below each category. For example, below *shirts* you might write *T-shirt, blouse*, and *button-down*; below *hats*, you might write *baseball cap, beret*, and *wool cap.*

2. Explain to students that they have just helped you make a network tree on the board. A network tree is used to organize data according to rank or importance (hierarchal ranking).

3. Give students a copy of the **Lots of Energy** and **Network Tree Organizer reproducibles (pages 33–34)**. Tell the class they will be working together to complete a network tree with facts from the "Lots of Energy" article. Place a transparency of the Network Tree Organizer reproducible on the overhead projector. Point out the number and arrangement of the circles in the organizer.

4. Invite a volunteer to read aloud "Lots of Energy" while the rest of the class listens. Then ask students: *What is the topic of this article?* Write the topic *energy* in the top oval of the network tree while students do the same on their paper.

5. Continue asking students questions to elicit the correct responses for the network tree.

For example: *Why are there two ovals below the top oval? What two kinds of energy are mentioned in the article?* (kinetic energy, potential energy) *Why are four ovals connected to each of those ovals on the chart? What should we write in the ovals connected to **kinetic energy** on the chart?* (electrical, radiant, thermal, mechanical) *What should we write in the ovals connected to **potential energy**?* (gravitational, nuclear, elastic, chemical)

6. Check students' work and their understanding of how to organize hierarchal data. Then point out the final rows of ovals at the bottom of the organizer. Tell students to write two examples of each kind of energy. They can work independently or with a partner. Provide a variety of science resources as needed.

   Electrical: electricity, lightning
   Radiant: visible light, sunlight, x-rays
   Thermal: hydrothermal, geothermal, solar
   Mechanical: wind, sound
   Gravitational: hydropower, Earth's gravity
   Nuclear: fission, fusion
   Elastic: compressed spring, stretched rubber band
   Chemical: natural gas, propane

7. After students are finished, invite them to share and compare their results with each other.

Extended Learning

- Have students consider how a network tree organizer might be used to show life science or earth science data. Ask them to brainstorm and share their ideas.

- Ask the class to search for examples of a network tree in newspapers or magazines. Mention that a network tree is a traditional way of showing family relationships starting with a single ancestor.

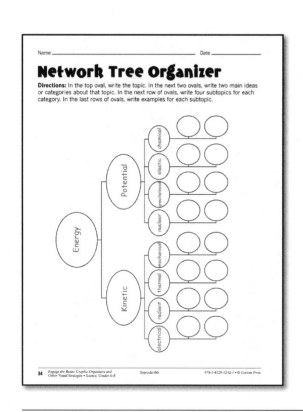

Lots of Energy

You can't see energy, but you can experience evidence of it through such things as motion, heat, sound, and light. **Energy** is the ability to do work, and **work** is the application of force through a distance. In other words, energy is what makes things happen. Need an example? Let's take the sun. The sun is made up of gases that take up space. These gases are matter. The sun gives off heat, which doesn't take up space but can do work, such as make you warm. Heat is a form of energy. (To be exact, it's the result of a transfer of energy.) The sun's light is also a form of energy. There are many forms of energy, but energy can be neither created nor destroyed. Energy can only change from one form to another.

All forms of energy can be grouped into two major categories: kinetic energy and potential energy. **Kinetic energy** involves any kind of motion. Electrical energy, thermal energy, radiant energy, and mechanical energy are all forms of kinetic energy. Examples include lightning, heat, light, wind, and sound. **Potential energy** is stored energy, or energy that is waiting to happen. Chemical energy, nuclear energy, elastic energy, and gravitational energy are usually sources of potential energy. Examples include natural gas, nuclear fission, a stretched rubber band, and an elevated object.

At any given time, an object can have kinetic energy or potential energy or both. For example, a ball at the top of a staircase has potential energy until it falls and then it has kinetic energy. A flowing river has kinetic energy until it is trapped behind a dam, at which time it has potential energy.

Network Tree Organizer

Directions: In the top oval, write the topic. In the next two ovals, write two main ideas or categories about that topic. In the next row of ovals, write four subtopics for each category. In the last rows of ovals, write examples for each subtopic.

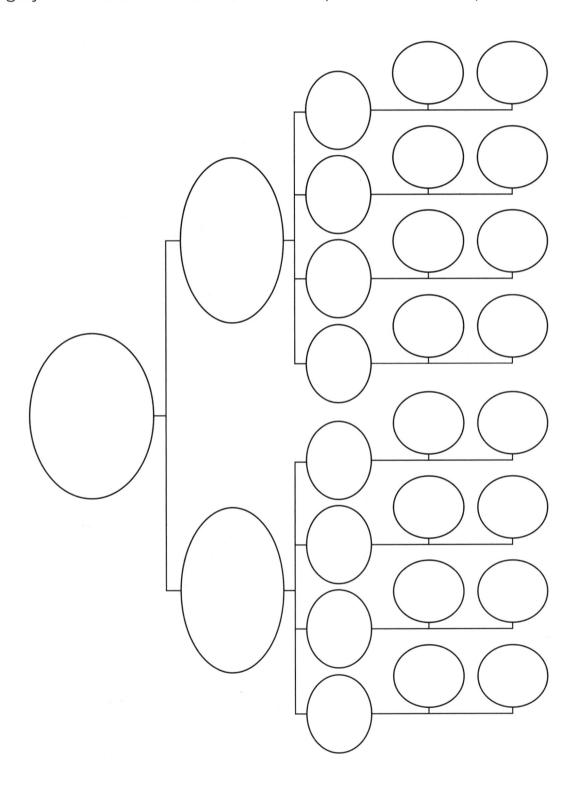

Heat Transfer: Demonstration and Project Planner

Skills Objectives
Discover relationships.
Evaluate and organize data.
Analyze information.

Materials
Science Project
Planner reproducible

penny

metal spoon and
plastic spoon of
equal size

margarine

shelled peanuts

boiling water

glass beaker or
measuring cup

A classroom **Demonstration** need not be elaborate to have an impact on learning. There are many ways that a demonstration can support the process of scientific inquiry and increase student retention. By contributing to group discussion and thinking aloud, students can experience the process of scientific inquiry firsthand. To help the demonstration run smoothly, keep it as simple as possible, use a **Project Planner**, explain each step along the way, ask students for comments and predictions, and address any safety concerns before you begin.

1. Tell students that you will be performing a simple demonstration to show how heat can transfer from one object to another. Hold up a penny, and say you want to warm it. Have students suggest a variety of ways to do so, such as: *Put the penny inside your closed fist; put it in sunlight; put it under a lamp.* Try any and all reasonable methods students suggest, and discuss the results.

2. Then demonstrate that some materials conduct heat better than others. First, lay a plastic spoon and a metal spoon flat on a demo table. Invite a volunteer to place a small, pea-sized dollop of margarine at the top of each handle and place a peanut in the center of each dollop.

3. Next, pour about an inch of boiling water into a beaker or measuring cup, keeping the steam away from the spoons. Ask students to predict what will happen when you put the bottom of the spoons (scoop end down) into the boiling water. Ask: *Will the margarine at the top melt? Which spoon do you think will transfer the heat better?* Have students explain their answers.

4. Conduct the demonstration, placing both spoons into the water at the same time. Allow students to comment or ask questions. The margarine on the metal spoon should heat faster; the peanut at the top of that spoon should fall first.

5. Encourage students to discuss what they observed. Ask if anyone has a suggestion for improving the demonstration, and try one of

their suggestions. Lead students to conclude that metal is a better heat conductor than plastic.

6. Distribute the **Science Project Planner reproducible (page 37)**. Divide the class into small groups, and instruct each group to use the reproducible to plan their own demonstration showing transfer of energy in any form.

7. When the plans are complete, allow time for each group to share their project planner with the class and perform their demonstration.

Extended Learning

- Invite a guest expert to do a demonstration for the class and discuss the benefits of a career in science.

- If you have access to a video camera, have students produce a video science demonstration. Play it for the class, or post it on your school Web site.

- Working with younger children can increase the confidence and self-esteem of older students and improve their communication skills. Divide the class into four groups, and have each group design a science demonstration to present to a younger class.

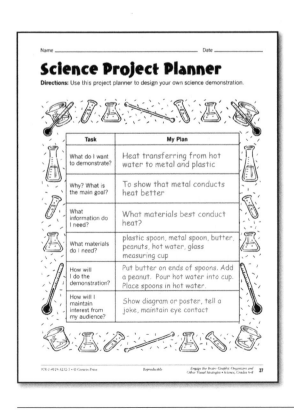

Name _____ Date _____

Science Project Planner

Directions: Use this project planner to design your own science demonstration.

Task	My Plan
What do I want to demonstrate?	Heat transferring from hot water to metal and plastic
Why? What is the main goal?	To show that metal conducts heat better
What information do I need?	What materials best conduct heat?
What materials do I need?	plastic spoon, metal spoon, butter, peanuts, hot water, glass measuring cup
How will I do the demonstration?	Put butter on ends of spoons. Add a peanut. Pour hot water into cup. Place spoons in hot water.
How will I maintain interest from my audience?	Show diagram or poster, tell a joke, maintain eye contact

Science Project Planner

Directions: Use this project planner to design your own science demonstration.

Task	My Plan
What do I want to demonstrate?	
Why? What is the main goal?	
What information do I need?	
What materials do I need?	
How will I do the demonstration?	
How will I maintain interest from my audience?	

CHAPTER 2

Life Science

Animal Characteristics: Triple Venn Diagram

Skills Objectives

Compare and contrast data.

Analyze information.

Discover relationships.

Use prior knowledge.

A **Venn Diagram** is a graphic organizer that helps students compare and contrast information. In the course of a life science unit, this organizer can be useful when students must compare physical characteristics, animal behavior, populations of plants, or types of ecosystems. Insights gathered by using a Venn diagram can lead to a deeper understanding of the living world.

1. Introduce the concept of "compare and contrast" by holding up two similar objects, such as a textbook and a blank notebook. Ask: *How are they alike?* (Both are paper; both have pages; both have covers.) *How are they different?* (Notebooks are blank and textbooks are not; you write in a notebook, not in a textbook.)

2. Tell students that they are going to use a Venn diagram to compare and contrast reptiles and amphibians. Initiate a discussion by asking students what they already know about reptiles and amphibians. Discuss the physical as well as behavioral traits of both animals. For example:

Reptile Characteristics	Amphibian Characteristics
Has a backbone	Has a backbone
Covered with scales	No scales
Cold-blooded	Cold-blooded
Often lays eggs on land	Often lays eggs in or near water
Breathes through lungs	May breathe through skin
Usually has claws	No claws
No larval stage	Has larval and adult stages
Never has gills	May have gills as baby or adult

3. Draw a Venn diagram (two large, overlapping circles) on the board to model its use for students. Label the left circle *Amphibians*

and the right circle *Reptiles*. Tell students they will write how amphibians and reptiles are alike in the overlapping section of the diagram. Ask: *What characteristics do they have in common?* List students' correct responses in that section of the diagram.

4. Work with students to list contrasting characteristics in the outer circles of the diagram. For example: *Reptiles—have scales; always breathe through lungs; lay eggs on land. Amphibians—don't have scales; sometimes breathe through their skin; lay eggs in or near water.*

5. Allow time for students to ask questions, making sure they understand how to record information on the diagram. Then give students a copy of the **Comparing Animals reproducible (page 40)**, and have them compare and contrast three types of animals on their own, such as a bat, bird, and snake; dog, wolf, and fox; squid, jellyfish, and sea star; or spider, scorpion, and ant. They can compare specific animals or animal groups.

6. After students complete their Venn diagrams, invite volunteers to share their results with the class. You may also choose to pair up students for a peer review.

Extended Learning

- Suggest that students draw a picture of each animal in their Venn diagram. Encourage them to include as many details as possible.

- Have students use a Venn diagram to compare and contrast different environments, such as desert, forest, and tundra.

- Have students research the different ways animals and humans detect and make use of their environment. As a class, create a Venn diagram to show the results.

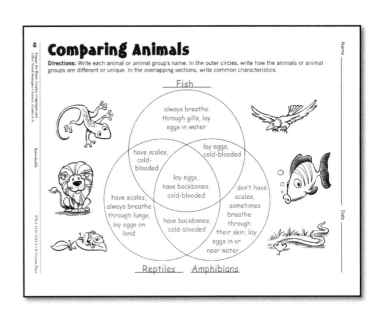

Comparing Animals

Directions: Write each animal or animal group's name. In the outer circles, write how the animals or animal groups are different or unique. In the overlapping sections, write common characteristics.

Engage the Brain: Graphic Organizers and Other Visual Strategies • Science, Grades 6–8   Reproducible   978-1-4129-5232-3 • © Corwin Press

Form and Function: Word Wall and Word Map

Skills Objectives

Use context clues and prior knowledge to find word meaning.
Access visual information quickly.

Materials

Form and Function
Word Map
reproducible

diagram of a
plant cell

glue

cardstock or poster
board

pushpins

A **Word Wall** is an excellent visual learning cue for students. Among its many advantages are its access and flexibility. Words can be attached using Velcro or pushpins, making it easier for students to move and rearrange them. Word walls are most effective when done as a whole group activity throughout the year. To make the most of a word wall, demonstrate its use and refer to it often. For science vocabulary, list words in logical categories, such as life science, physical science, and earth science. If you don't have enough space for a word wall, use a freestanding display board that can be put up and taken down as needed.

1. Tell the class they will be working together to create a science word wall of important terms and definitions. Explain that a word wall is an expanding display of words that can be used as a reference throughout the year.

2. Begin the activity by showing students a large diagram of a plant cell, and have volunteers help you label the important parts, such as: *cell membrane, cell wall, chloroplast, cytoplasm, Golgi body, mitochondrion, nucleolus, nucleus, ribosome, endoplasmic reticulum, stroma, vacuole*. Then tell students they will be completing word maps about these terms to put on the science word wall.

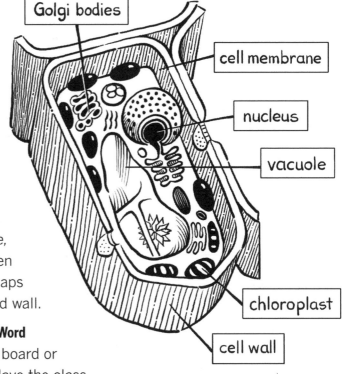

3. Give students a copy of the **Form and Function Word Map reproducible (page 43)**. Draw a copy on the board or reproduce it on an overhead transparency. Have the class help you complete your word map for the word *nucleus*. Write *nucleus* on the flask in the middle of the diagram, and ask: *What is the definition of* **nucleus**? (the central part of a cell that controls many of the cell's activities) Write the answer in the box labeled *Definition*.

4. Ask a volunteer to give a physical description of a nucleus. *(dense area surrounded by a nuclear membrane and containing the nucleolus and chromatin)* Write the correct response in the box labeled *Description*, and draw a simple picture to go with it.

5. For the box labeled *Function*, elicit from students an explanation, such as *controls protein synthesis.* For the box labeled *Details*, ask students to describe a *nucleus,* such as *contains DNA,* and record their responses.

6. Review the completed word map with students, and answer any questions about it. Then assign or have students choose one of the other science terms from the diagram or from a current science lesson to complete their own Form and Function Word Map reproducible.

7. Give students time to share and discuss their completed word maps with the rest of the class. Laminate the completed word maps or glue them onto cardstock for durability before posting them on the word wall in alphabetical order.

8. Encourage students to add new vocabulary to the word wall as you progress through your current unit and continue on with other units throughout the year.

Extended Learning

- After the word wall has been up for about a week, take the words down and challenge students to recall the words and the definitions. Put the words back on the wall as they are identified.

- Play "mystery word" by removing one of the words from the word wall and asking students to determine which one is missing.

- Divide the class into two teams. Remove the words from the wall. Read the definition of a word, and have teams take turns trying to guess the word.

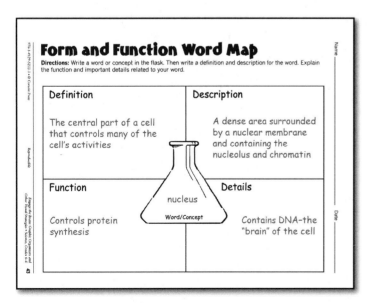

Name _____ Date _____

Form and Function Word Map

Directions: Write a word or concept in the beaker. Then write a definition and description for the word. Explain the function and important details related to your word.

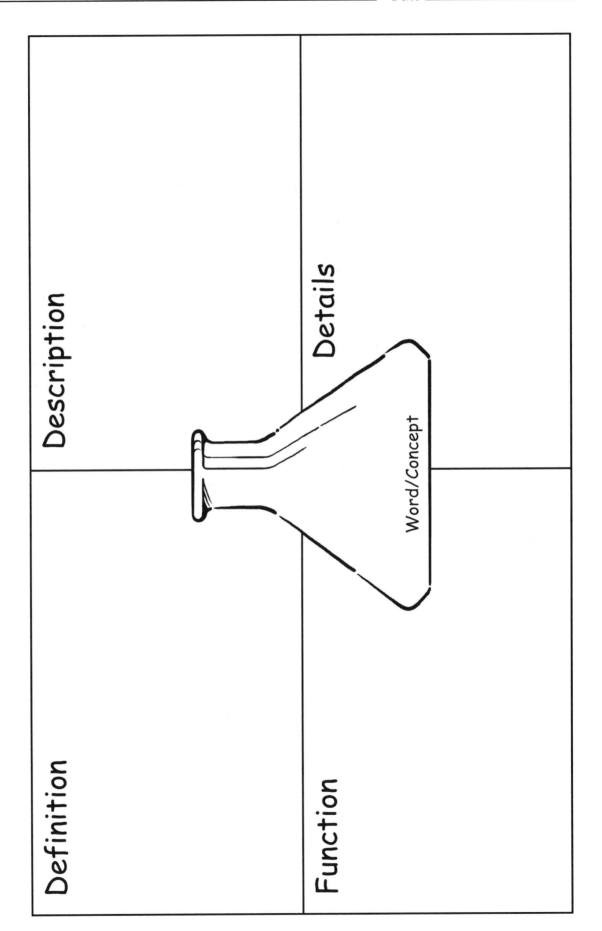

Definition	Description
Function	**Details**

Word/Concept

Observation and Inference: T-Chart

Materials

Observation and Inference reproducible

apple

pencil

clipboards

Skills Objectives

Compare and contrast information.

Distinguish between observations and inferences.

A **T-Chart** enables students to list information about two objects and then graphically compare, contrast, and clarify their understanding of those objects. Objects, or topics, may be examined in a variety of ways, such as: *advantages and disadvantages, pros and cons, problems and solutions, cause and effect, fact and opinion*, or *before and after*. A T-chart is particularly useful in science when comparing and contrasting terms that students sometimes confuse.

1. In advance, take a bite out of an apple and put a pencil hole in the opposite side. Save the apple for later in the lesson.

2. Explain to students that science is based on observation and inference. Ask volunteers to share what they know about making observations and inferences. Then explain that an *observation* is the action of using the senses to gain information, whereas an *inference* is a conclusion based on evidence or reasoning about something already observed. Inferences may not always result in the correct conclusion.

3. To illustrate the difference between an observation and an inference, draw a sad face with tears on the board. Ask students: *What do you observe about this face?* (tears, frown) *What can you infer about how this person is feeling? Why?* (The person is sad; the person is crying and looks unhappy.) Then change the frown to a smile. Ask: *Would you still infer that the person is sad? Why or why not?* (No; the smile indicates that the tears might be tears of joy.) Point out that the inference is based on observation, prior knowledge, and speculation.

4. Draw a T-chart on the board. Title the left column *Observations*, and the right column *Inferences*. Explain that students are going to help you complete a T-chart listing observations and inferences about an apple.

 978-1-4129-5232-3

5. Display the apple with the bite side facing students (keep the hole hidden). Ask: *What do you observe about the apple?* (Answers might include: *It is red, shiny, smooth, round, and small; someone has taken a bite out of it.*) Record their observations on the T-chart. Then ask: *What inferences can you make based on your observations?* (The apple is probably hard, sweet, and ripe. A person took a bite out of it.) Record their inferences on the T-chart.

6. Then turn the apple to show the hole. Ask students: *What do you observe now?* (There's a hole in the apple.) *What are some possible inferences?* (Someone or something put a hole in the apple.) *What if you saw a worm next to the apple? What might you infer?* (The worm made the hole in the apple.)

7. Discuss the importance of distinguishing between observations and inferences. Ask: *How do you think both are used in science? Why are they both important?* Help students understand that scientists first observe and then use inferences to explain their observations. Scientists must then prove that their inferences are correct.

8. Give each student a clipboard and a copy of the **Observation and Inference reproducible (page 46)**. Review with students how to complete the reproducible, referring to the example on the board and checking for understanding.

9. Take students outdoors. For five minutes, have them record observations on their T-chart. Direct them to use their senses (sight, sound, smell, touch) to make observations about plants, animals, people, and objects in their environment. (They should not use people's names. They can refer to "a student" or "an adult.") Invite students to write inferences about what they observed.

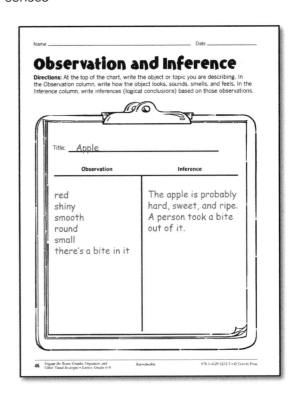

10. Invite students to share their results. Ask volunteers to share their observations while classmates make inferences about those observations. Then have volunteers share their inferences.

Extended Learning

- Have students read a magazine article about an animal. Ask them to underline information clearly based on observation and to circle inferences.

- Lead a discussion about how prior knowledge and observations can help a scientist make predictions.

Observation and Inference

Directions: At the top of the chart, write the object or topic you are describing. In the *Observation* column, write how the object looks, sounds, smells, and feels. In the *Inference* column, write inferences (logical conclusions) based on those observations.

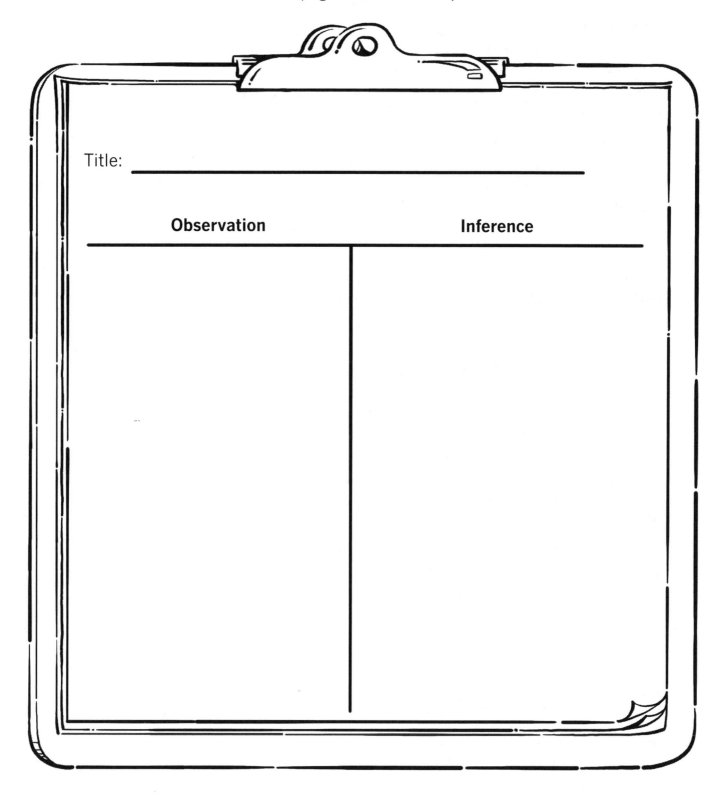

Title: _____

Observation	Inference

Life Cycles: Cycle Chart

Skills Objectives
Identify main ideas.
Understand a sequence of events.
Understand a repetitive cycle.

Materials

Metamorphosis reproducible

Life Cycle Chart reproducible

colored pencils or markers

books and other resources about life cycles

A **Cycle Chart** is used in science to show a continuous or repetitive process. It gives a clear picture of the stages of the process and how it begins, ends, and repeats. Whether it is the cycle of metamorphosis, the carbon cycle, the water cycle, or any other cycle in nature, this kind of chart helps students to focus on key elements and understand how each stage is important to the process.

1. To show the repetitive process of a cycle, have students think about a day in their own lives. Ask: *What do you do every day? What is your daily routine?* (Possible answers: *wake up, get dressed, eat breakfast, go to school, study, have lunch, study more, go home, see friends, do homework, eat dinner, watch TV, go to bed*) Write a daily routine on the board in the form of a cycle chart.

2. Brainstorm with students a list of other cycles in nature (e.g., *water cycle, cycle of a day from sunrise to sunrise, yearly cycle of the seasons, life cycle*). Then give students a copy of the **Metamorphosis** and **Cycle Chart reproducibles (pages 49–50)**. Draw a simple cycle chart on the board. Explain to students that they will be helping you complete a cycle chart using information from the "Metamorphosis" article.

3. Have volunteers read aloud "Metamorphosis" as the rest of the class listens. Ask students: *What is the first stage of complete metamorphosis?* (egg) Ask a volunteer to write and draw the first stage of the cycle on the board. Continue the process for each stage of development (egg, larva, pupa, adult) until the cycle chart is complete. Then ask: *How is this cycle different from incomplete metamorphosis?* Refer students to the dragonfly cycle in the article.

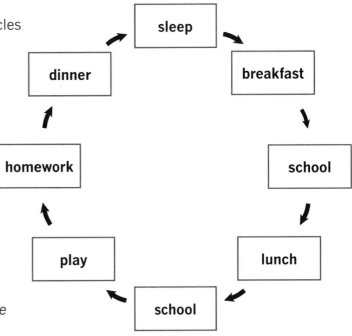

4. Refer students to their Cycle Chart reproducible. Tell them to complete a chart of another insect or other living thing and to include drawings. They may draw more boxes and arrows as needed to complete their chart. Provide students with science books and other resources to help them complete their charts. Encourage students to include other details as well, such as the duration of time for each stage of the cycle.

5. When cycle charts are finished, display them in the classroom for students to examine, compare, and assess.

Extended Learning

- Ask students what they know about caterpillars, maggots, and grubs. Each of these is a stage in the cycle of metamorphosis. Have the class research and learn which insect and which stage these examples are from.

- Create a butterfly display in the classroom so students can observe metamorphosis in action.

- Have students create posters of different cycles in nature. Encourage them to include magazine cutouts, computer graphics, and three-dimensional artwork.

- Explain that insect extermination sometimes includes the use of substances that interrupt the egg-laying cycle. Ask how and why such an approach is successful.

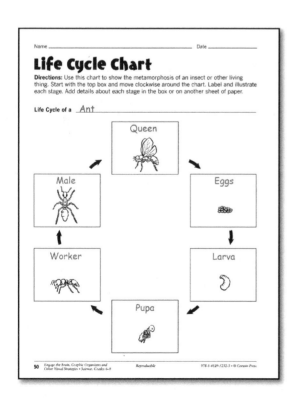

Metamorphosis

Most insects develop in four stages. This is called **metamorphosis**. During this process, insects change from eggs to adults.

A typical life cycle starts with the egg, which hatches into a larva. The larva is an eating machine that molts its skin as it grows larger and larger. Then it pupates, or stops eating, and enters a resting stage. An insect may be in the resting stage for a short time, over an entire season, or even longer. Finally, the insect emerges as an adult. This kind of development is called **complete metamorphosis**, in which the insect looks very different from one stage to the next.

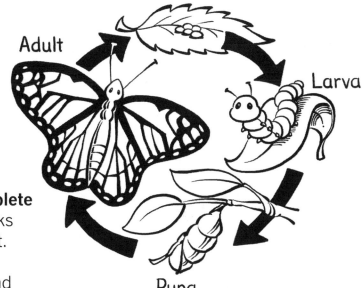

Some insects, such as dragonflies and crickets, go through **incomplete metamorphosis**. They hatch from the egg as a nymph, which often looks a lot like the adult without wings. The insect grows larger, molts several times, and eventually develops wings. Once the insect stops growing, it has become an adult.

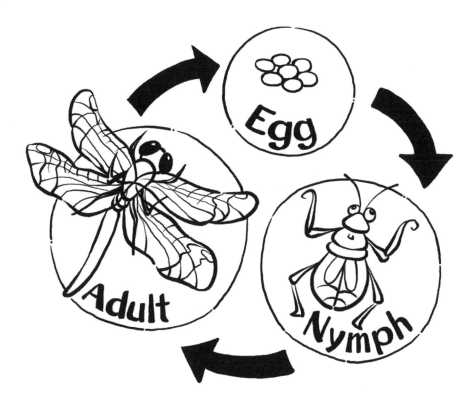

Life Cycle Chart

Directions: Use this chart to show the metamorphosis of an insect or other living thing. Start with the top box, and move clockwise around the chart. Label and illustrate each stage. Add details about stages in the box or on another sheet of paper.

Life Cycle of a _____

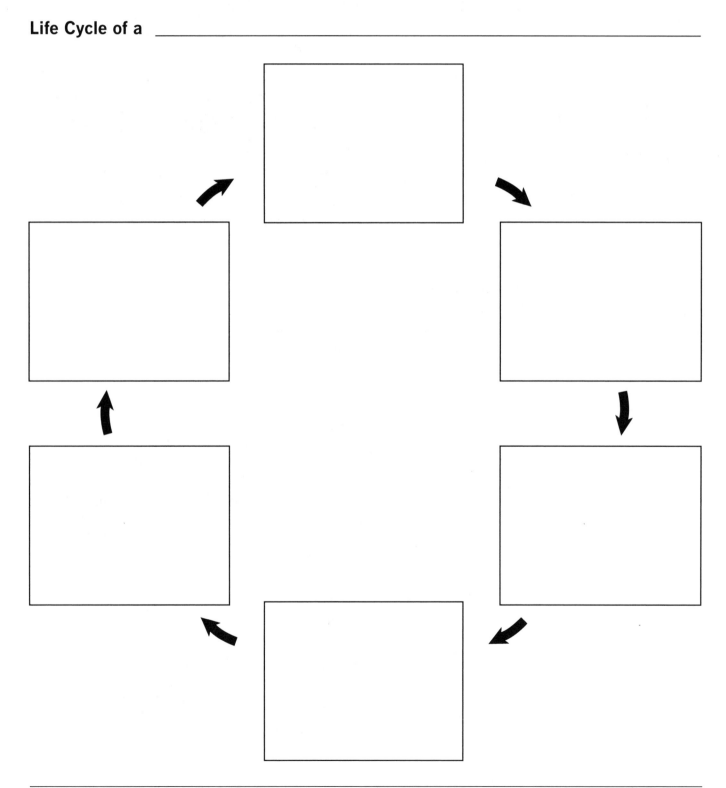

Food Web: Flowchart

Skills Objectives
Understand hierarchal relationships in nature.
Illustrate trends.
Examine patterns.
Predict outcomes.

Materials

Food Web Flowchart reproducible

overhead projector and transparency

Flowcharts, storyboards, and chain of events maps are all useful organizers in showing progression that is linear rather than cyclical. The **Flowchart**, however, is easily customized to list and describe stages of development, such as the natural growth of a forest or the recovery of a forest after a forest fire. Using a flowchart is an excellent way to show linear progression in nature from beginning to end.

1. To show a logical progression to the class, prompt students to describe how vegetables get from the farm to their kitchen table, and write their ideas in linear sequence on the board. For example: *Vegetables are picked and put in boxes. Boxes are loaded onto trucks and taken to the store. The store sells vegetables and consumers buy them. Vegetables are brought home and eaten.* Point out that this is only one possible pathway from production to consumption.

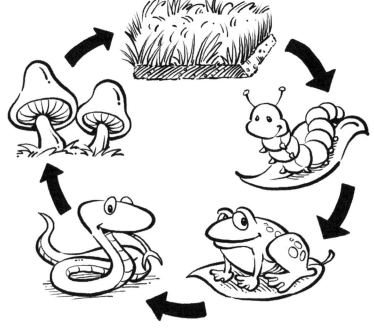

2. Give students a copy of the **Food Web Flowchart reproducible (page 53)**, and place a transparency of the flowchart on an overhead projector. Tell students they will use the flowchart to explore how energy is transferred between living things. Then ask them to share what they already know about food chains and food webs.

3. Model how to complete the flowchart, illustrating it step by step on the transparency as students follow along on their papers. Write the topic *Transfer of Energy*. Ask students: *What is the primary source of energy for all living things on the planet?* Write *sun* in the box labeled *Primary Source*.

4. Then point out the first row of boxes labeled *Producer*. Explain to students that a *producer* uses energy from the sun to produce

its own food through photosynthesis. Ask: *What is another name for **producer**?* (autotroph) Then ask: *What kinds of living things produce their own food?* (plants) Have students suggest three different plants to write in the boxes and choose their own plants for their flowcharts.

5. Point out the next row of boxes labeled *Primary Consumer*. Ask students to define the word *primary* (first) and the word *consumer* (eater). Point out that all primary consumers are plant-eaters. Ask: *What is the scientific name for **plant eater**?* (herbivore) Have students suggest three different herbivores to write in the boxes and choose their own herbivores for their flowcharts. Point out that all consumers are *heterotrophs*—they do not produce their own food the way autotrophs do.

6. Repeat the process for the next row of boxes labeled *Secondary Consumer*. Explain that all secondary consumers are meat eaters. Ask students: *What is the scientific name for an animal that eats other animals?* (carnivore) *What is the scientific name for an animal that eats both plants and animals?* (omnivore) Have students suggest three different carnivores or omnivores to write in the boxes and choose their own animals to write in their flowcharts.

7. The last box is labeled *Decomposer*. Ask students: *What is the job of a decomposer?* (to break down the remains of dead material into simpler nutrients that are absorbed in the soil and reused by plants) Ask students to suggest a decomposer for the last box, such as *fungi* or *worms*.

8. When students are finished, invite them to share and compare their results. Discuss the similarities and differences in their food webs.

Extended Learning

Energy is lost as it passes through a food chain. Ask students to research and report their findings as to why this happens and determine why there are fewer large predators than small primary consumers.

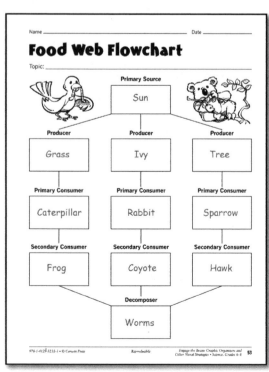

Name _____ Date _____

Food Web Flowchart

Topic: _____

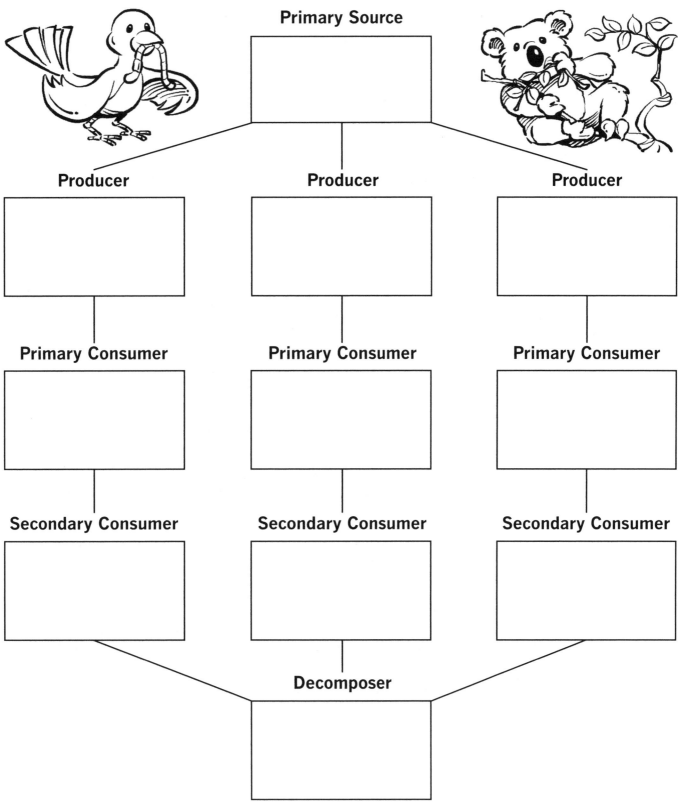

Primary Source

Producer

Producer

Producer

Primary Consumer

Primary Consumer

Primary Consumer

Secondary Consumer

Secondary Consumer

Secondary Consumer

Decomposer

Five Senses: Field Trip and Sensory Chart

Materials

Sensory Chart reproducible

colored pencils

sketch pad (optional)

camera (optional)

Skills Objectives

Analyze information.

Evaluate relationships in nature.

Communicate data within a group.

Studying nature inside a classroom can't always accomplish the depth of understanding that an outdoor **Field Trip** can provide. To motivate your class, you needn't go further than a local park or a school garden. Direct interaction with science in the environment encourages students to apply prior knowledge to real-life experiences and thus improves retention and understanding of key concepts. Depending on your goals, a field trip may take place at any point during a study unit, although earlier in the unit often produces the best results.

1. Plan your trip with a specific goal in mind, and prepare students for the upcoming field trip. Explain where you will be going, why you are going, and what you expect students to accomplish. Design the field trip to support a particular unit of study, such as exploring ecosystems at a local park.

2. Begin your preparation by reviewing and discussing with students important terms they should know for the trip. For example, for a trip about ecosystems, remind students that an *ecosystem* is a biological community of organisms that interact with one another and their physical environment. Point out that an ecosystem may be as big as the entire park or as small as a fallen log and that it includes plant populations, animal populations, and nonliving components.

3. Give students a copy of the **Sensory Chart reproducible (page 56)**. Explain how to use the chart, pointing out the five boxes for each of the five senses. Encourage students to illustrate some observations if they prefer. You might also suggest that they bring along a camera and a sketch pad.

4. Divide the class into small groups, and have them work together during the field trip to gather and record information. Before you go, review proper conduct, and be certain students understand the purpose of the trip.

5. During the field trip, circulate among the groups to be sure that students understand the types of observations to record on their sensory chart. Offer suggestions, but give students plenty of opportunity to be creative and original.

6. When you return from the trip, allow time for students to discuss the most interesting aspects of their experience and share what they learned. Display their charts and any drawings or photographs on a bulletin board.

Extended Learning

• Bring along a tape recorder or video camera on your field trip. Interview students, or invite them to interview each other to share comments and observations. Play the tape back in class and use the comments as a springboard for discussion.

• Encourage each student to make a scrapbook of the field trip. The book could include a hand-drawn map, photos, drawings, and souvenir objects such as dried leaves. Display the finished scrapbooks in the classroom.

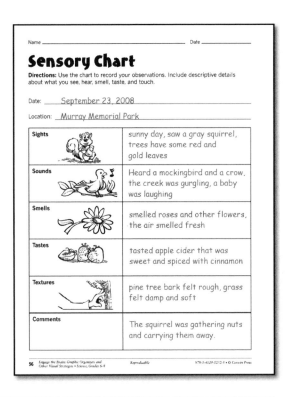

Name _____ Date _____

Sensory Chart

Directions: Use the chart to record your observations. Include descriptive details about what you see, hear, smell, taste, and touch.

Date: _____

Location: _____

Sights	
Sounds	
Smells	
Tastes	
Textures	
Comments	

Biomes: Extended Cluster Map

Skills Objectives
Read a map.
Recognize patterns.
Discover relationships.
Organize data.

Materials
Biomes reproducibles

Extended Cluster Map reproducible

colored pencils or markers

resources about biomes

overhead projector and transparency

An **Extended Cluster Map** is an excellent visual tool for displaying large amounts of data. It allows students to group together the elements of a unit that have similar, dependent, and sometimes overlapping features. The individual units can then be grouped to illustrate how they relate to each other as parts of a whole. The extended cluster map is ideal for showing Earth's biomes and their major features.

1. Write on the board *The World of Sports* and three subtitles: *Soccer Field, Swimming Pool,* and *Tennis Court.* Ask students to describe plants, animals, people, and other items usually found on a soccer field, and list their suggestions on the board. Repeat the process for a tennis court and a swimming pool. Point out the similarities and differences between the three sports communities.

2. Write *The World's Biosphere* on the board. Explain to students that Earth's biosphere is the entire region in which living things can be found, from deep in the ground to high in the sky. It is broken into *biomes,* or naturally occurring communities of plants and animals within a large habitat with a unique climate. There are five major biomes that make up distinct areas of the biosphere, each with a particular type of climate, soil, and population of living things.

3. Give students a copy of the **Biomes** and **Extended Cluster Map reproducibles (pages 59–60)**. Place a transparency of the Extended Cluster Map on the overhead projector. Write *Biomes* in the center oval and *Forest* in one of the five connecting ovals. Invite students to share what they know about forests, and name the three kinds of forests from their Biomes sheet. Write the names in the three connecting ovals of the extended cluster map as students follow along on their papers.

4. Repeat the process for the other four biomes, using different colored markers for each category. Have students do the same on their papers.

5. Point out the lines extending outward from each of the smaller ovals on the extended cluster map. Explain that those lines are for listing examples of plants and animals that live in each region. Work with students to name and record plants and animals that live in a rain forest, adding more lines if desired.

6. Invite students to work in pairs to research and record the names of organisms that live in the other biomes. Provide research materials and resources, including Internet access if possible. Monitor students' progress as they work, and offer assistance as needed.

7. Display students' completed extended cluster maps, and invite students to share what they learned. Take a poll to find out which biome students like the best.

Extended Learning

- Display a large sheet of butcher paper on the wall for each biome, and place a box below each one. Divide the class into small groups. Have students cut out magazine pictures of animals and decide together the best biome for each animal. After students place their pictures in the boxes, review the contents of each box with the class. Decide if the animals have been correctly placed. Then have students glue the pictures onto the corresponding biome. Encourage them to draw details to complete each display.

- Divide the class into small groups, and have each group choose a subcategory from the outer ovals of their biome cluster map, such as *fresh water*. Have them complete another cluster map, this time putting the name of that subcategory in the center and further dividing it into smaller subsections. For example, *fresh water* could be divided into *swamps*, *lakes*, *ponds*, and *rivers*.

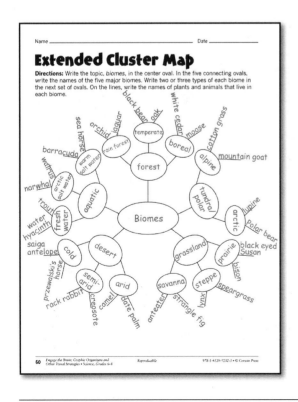

Biomes

FOREST
Rainforest
Temperate forest
Boreal forest (taiga)

DESERT
Arid deserts
Semi-arid deserts
Cold deserts

GRASSLAND
Prairie
Steppe
Savanna

TUNDRA/POLAR
Arctic
Alpine

AQUATIC
Warm salt water
Arctic salt water
Fresh water

Extended Cluster Map

Directions: Write the topic, *biomes*, in the center oval. In the five connecting ovals, write the names of the five major biomes. Write two or three types of each biome in the next set of ovals. On the lines, write the names of plants and animals that live in each biome.

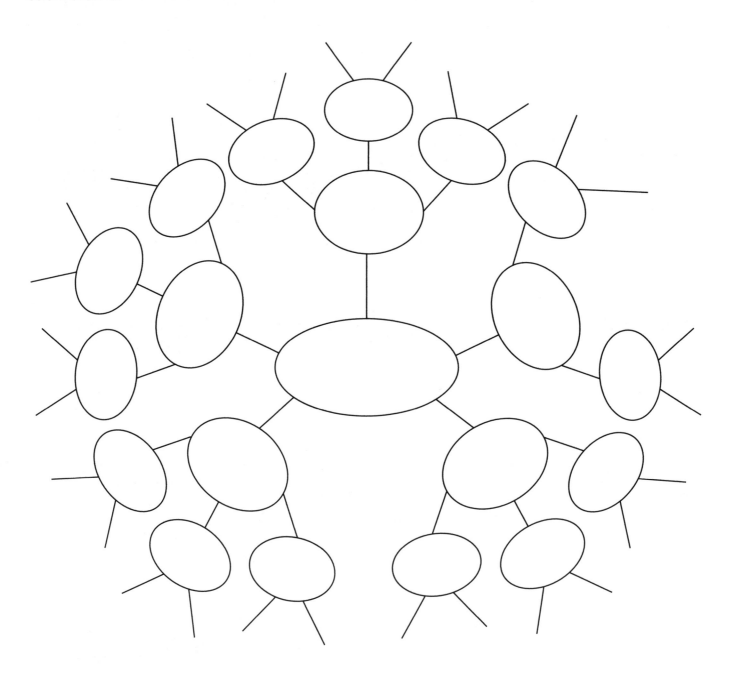

Ecosystems: Classroom Model and Comparison Chart

Skills Objectives

Use observation to predict behavior.
Collect and communicate data.
Compare and contrast data.
Recognize patterns.

Materials

Comparison Chart reproducible

terrarium

science journals

A **Classroom Model** of a living ecosystem, such as a terrarium or aquarium, is an ideal way to reach visual and kinesthetic learners. Although it can add to their learning, it isn't necessary for students to actually create the model themselves. Simply observing and interacting with a living ecosystem can engage a student's curiosity and lead to a deeper understanding of nature.

A terrarium is probably the least expensive and least labor-intensive ecosystem you can display in your classroom. You can purchase a terrarium, but it's also easy to make one. Use a large clear container, a bottom layer of gravel, some potting soil, a collection of seeds, live plants, and small animals such as worms, crickets, snails, and ants. Be sure to include some drinking water in a shallow dish or depression in the soil for the animals. You may also include a variety of colorful rocks and small twigs for visual appeal. Be sure the terrarium can be sealed with a lid to allow for an internal water cycle. Water vapor from the plants will keep the terrarium moist, and you will rarely have to water it. Place the terrarium where it will receive a few hours of partial sunlight every day.

1. Introduce students to the terrarium, and give them time to view it closely before starting the lesson. Encourage them to record their observations in science journals.

2. Explain that a terrarium is an example of a closed ecosystem. Draw a simple diagram of the terrarium on the board, and point out the different components. Ask students: *What are the nonliving components?* (sunlight, water, air, soil, rocks, twigs) *What are the living components?* Discuss the interaction and interdependence of the living and nonliving components within the terrarium.

3. Give students a copy of the **Comparison Chart reproducible (page 63)**. Tell them to select two of the living organisms in the terrarium to compare and contrast. Model how to complete the chart using a plant and a snail. Help students compare and contrast the physical characteristics, sources of food and water, defense mechanisms, reproduction, ecological relationships, and overall contributions of the plant and snail.

4. Monitor students as they work, checking for understanding and guiding them as needed. Encourage students to use descriptive details in their writing.

5. When students' charts are completed, display them on the wall next to the terrarium.

Extended Learning

- Have students predict and discuss what would happen to the equilibrium of the terrarium's ecosystem if one of the following changes occurred: using more or less water, using more or less sunlight, using artificial light instead of sunlight, adding a carnivorous plant such as a Venus flytrap.

- Encourage students to observe similar animals in their natural habitat and compare and contrast behavior. For example, how do snails in the terrarium behave differently than snails in the wild?

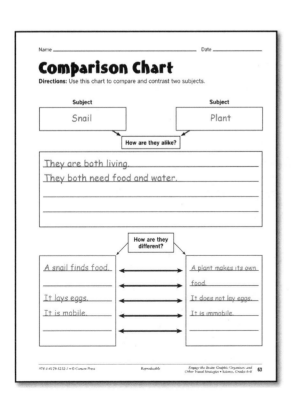

Name _____   Date _____

Comparison Chart

Directions: Use this chart to compare and contrast two subjects.

Subject   **Subject**

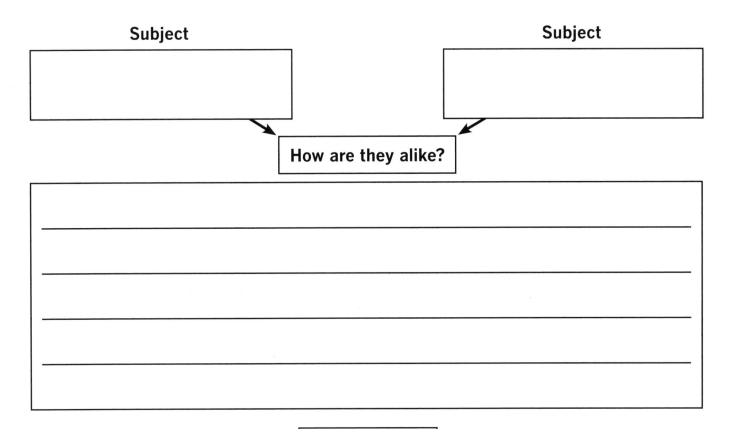

How are they alike?

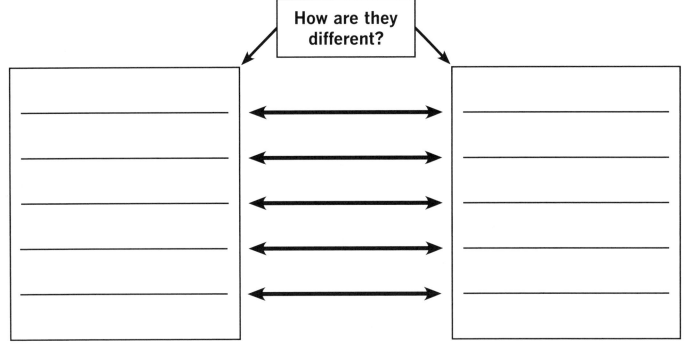

How are they different?

Endangered Species: Trading Cards

Materials

Species Trading Cards reproducible

research materials about endangered species

colored pencils

scissors

glue

cardstock or poster board

overhead projector and transparency

Skills Objectives

Understand the concept of extinction.

Read with a purpose.

Summarize data.

Trading Cards are a part of popular culture and so have a unique appeal to young students. They help students recall facts and details and summarize data. Creating cards offers students a fun way to demonstrate their knowledge, or show what they know. Because cards may be handmade or computer generated, they benefit students with a variety of learning styles.

1. Ask students if any of them collect trading cards. Invite volunteers to explain the components that make up the cards. Tell the class that they will be making their own trading cards about endangered animals.

2. Give students a copy of the **Species Trading Cards reproducible (page 66)**. Invite them to share what they already know about endangered animals and extinction. Ask students: *What's the difference between an endangered species and an extinct species? What are some ways that an animal can become endangered or extinct?* (loss of habitat, hunting, interruption of breeding cycle, disease) *What can we do to help endangered animals?*

3. Place a transparency of the Trading Cards reproducible on the overhead projector. Work with students to create a sample card about the giant panda. Draw a simple picture of a giant panda on the top portion of the card. Tell students they will need to research the animal's habitat, range, population in the wild, lifespan, size, diet, and main threat (reason why the animal is endangered).

Encourage students to guess information about the giant panda before you write it on the transparency.

> **Panda Facts**
> **Name:** Giant panda
> **Habitat:** Bamboo and coniferous forests
> **Range:** Szechuan, Shensi, and Kansu provinces in central and western China
> **Wild Population:** Approximately 1,000
> **Lifespan:** In captivity, pandas can live 20 years.
> **Size:** Up to 3 feet tall, 6 feet long, and 250 pounds
> **Diet:** Mainly bamboo
> **Main Threat:** Habitat loss

4. Have students create four trading cards for four animals. Ask them to select a variety of animals and environments, such as a mammal, a bird, a reptile, and an insect from different parts of the world. Have them use at least three resources to confirm facts, including books, magazines, and Web sites such as Kids Planet at: *www.kidsplanet.org/factsheets/map.html* and the U.S. Fish and Wildlife Endangered Species Page at: *www.fws.gov/endangered*.

5. Have students glue their cards onto a cardstock or poster board backing for durability. You might also laminate the cards or use clear contact paper. Remind students to write their name on the back of each card before laminating it.

6. Invite each student to share facts about one endangered animal, or collect all of the cards and redistribute them for students to read and share information. You might also play a class game, having students read facts about a mystery animal, while classmates try to guess the animal's identity.

Extended Learning

- Explain to students that there are many endangered plants as well as animals. Suggest that they design trading cards about endangered plants.

- Have student groups create a rescue plan for a particular plant or animal.

- Ask students to bring in magazine and newspaper articles about conservation groups that focus on saving endangered plants or animals. Create a bulletin board or book of the articles.

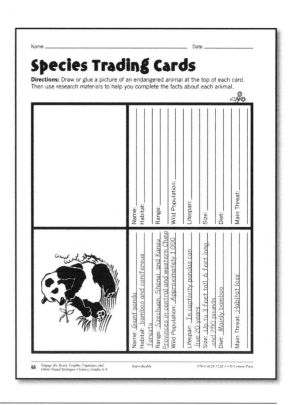

Name ______________________ Date ____________

Species Trading Cards

Directions: Draw or glue a picture of an endangered animal at the top of each card. Then use research materials to help you complete the facts about each animal.

Name: ____________
Habitat: ____________
Range: ____________
Wild Population: ____________
Lifespan: ____________
Size: ____________
Diet: ____________
Main Threat: ____________

Name: ____________
Habitat: ____________
Range: ____________
Wild Population: ____________
Lifespan: ____________
Size: ____________
Diet: ____________
Main Threat: ____________

Reproducible

CHAPTER 3

Earth Science

Portrait of Earth: Poster

Skills Objectives

Access multiple sources of information.

Evaluate and organize data.

Present information clearly.

Materials

Portrait of Earth reproducible

rulers

poster board

art supplies

A picture is worth a thousand words. **Posters** in the classroom are a visually appealing way to present tables, graphs, charts, and maps to students. They provide detailed information in bite-sized pieces, making it easier for students to understand and communicate key information about a given topic.

1. Point out various posters you have displayed in the classroom. Ask students to quickly identify the information on some of the posters and describe its purpose. Then tell students that they will be making a poster to show Earth at a glance.

2. Demonstrate by working with students to design a sample poster of one feature of Earth—the atmosphere. First, write the five atmospheric layers on the board in random order. Ask students: *What is the correct order of atmospheric layers, from lowest to outermost layer?* (troposphere, stratosphere, mesosphere, thermosphere, exosphere) Encourage students to share what they already know about Earth's atmosphere by asking questions such as: *In which layer does most of Earth's weather occur?* (troposphere) *Which inner layer is coldest?* (mesosphere)

3. Draw a large rectangle on the board to represent a poster, and ask students to help you sketch a design. Ask a volunteer to draw a strip at the bottom of the poster and label it *Earth*. Discuss how to determine the thickness of the atmospheric layers if they are drawn to scale. Suggest the following: troposphere–1/4 inch, stratosphere and mesosphere–1/2 inch each, thermosphere–6 1/2 inches. Invite volunteers to use a ruler to draw and label each layer above *Earth*.

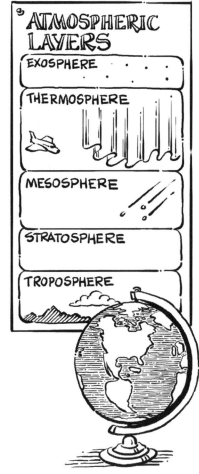

Layers of Earth's Atmosphere

Troposphere (0 to 10 miles): Most of Earth's weather occurs in this layer.

Stratosphere (10 to 30 miles): The ozone is found within this layer.

Mesosphere (30 to 50 miles): The temperature drops quickly in this layer.

Thermosphere (50 to 300 miles): The air heats up again due to solar radiation.

Exosphere (300 miles and beyond): The outermost layer of the atmosphere. The exosphere is extremely thin and is made up of scattered atoms of hydrogen, oxygen, and helium.

4. Brainstorm other details to add to the poster to make it more visually appealing. For example, ask: *How could we show that weather takes place in the thermosphere? How could we show a jet stream between the troposphere and the stratosphere? What about showing the ozone layer between the stratosphere and the mesosphere?* Students could add more interest to the poster by posting facts about the atmospheric layers. Point out that large text, interesting fonts, and colorful diagrams are effective communication tools.

5. Divide the class into small groups, and give students a copy of the **Portrait of Earth reproducible (page 69)**. Explain that the organizer is for recording facts about Earth for their poster. Encourage students to use a variety of research materials to gather facts.

6. Help students generate a list of materials for their poster. Encourage them to include artwork, photographs, diagrams, three-dimensional features, and other visuals to make their poster more interesting. Tell them to draw a design sketch of their poster and get your approval before making it.

7. Create a classroom display of students' finished posters, or post them in an outdoor hallway. Invite groups to review each other's work.

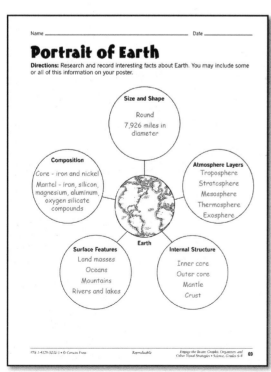

Name _____ Date _____

Portrait of Earth

Directions: Research and record interesting facts about Earth. You may include some or all of this information on your poster.

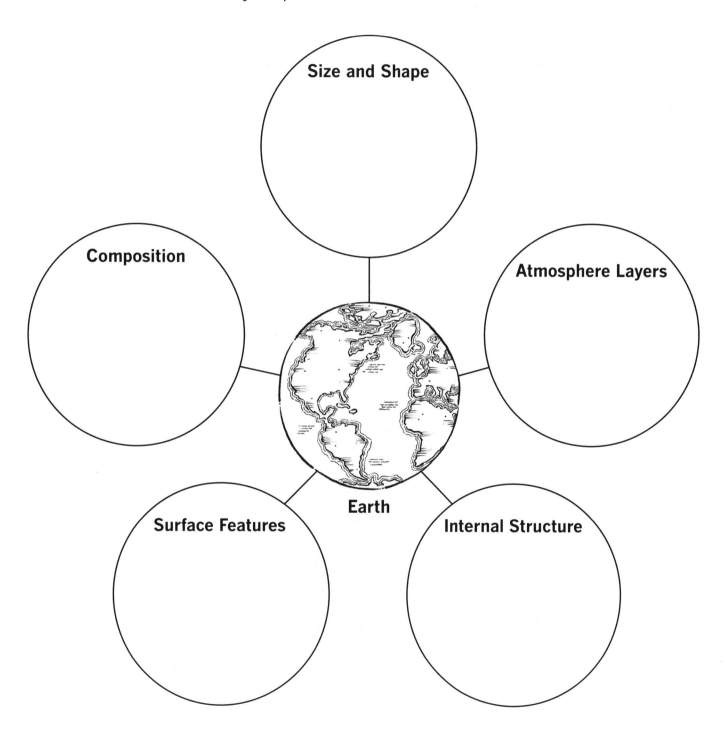

Size and Shape

Composition

Atmosphere Layers

Surface Features

Earth

Internal Structure

Precipitation: Concept Map

Materials

Precipitation reproducible

Concept Map reproducible

research materials about precipitation

art supplies

Skills Objectives

Present information orally.

Evaluate and organize data.

A simple **Concept Map** is used to show a snapshot of a main topic and a variety of elements that relate to that topic. For students, the act of creating the map and entering the data clarifies the information and leads to better understanding and retention. Using a simple concept map is also an effective note-taking strategy.

1. Draw a simple concept map on the board or on an overhead transparency. Explain to students that a concept map can be used to show facts and ideas related to a specific topic.

2. Ask students to define *precipitation. (any form of water, solid or liquid that falls from clouds and reaches Earth's surface)* Write *precipitation* in the center of the map, and ask students to name seven different types of precipitation. Record correct responses in the surrounding circles. *(rain, drizzle, sleet, freezing rain, hail, snowflakes, snow pellets)*

3. Gives students a copy of the **Precipitation** and **Concept Map reproducibles (pages 72–73)**. Explain that they will be completing their own concept map about one form of precipitation, researching facts for the surrounding circles, and then presenting a brief oral report about that form of precipitation.

4. Have volunteers take turns reading aloud the descriptions of precipitation on the reproducible. Then have students choose the form of precipitation they'd like to research and write that name in the center of their concept map.

5. Use the concept map on the board to model a brief oral report based on the information shown. For example, define *precipitation* and give one or two facts about each type to show how the map can be used as an outline. Tell students they may refer to their completed map during their oral report.

6. Provide students with research materials. Encourage them to practice their oral reports before presenting them in class. Remind students to speak slowly and clearly and to make eye contact during their presentation.

7. Allow class time for students to present their oral reports. Display the completed concept maps on a bulletin board, and encourage students to add decorative artwork.

Extended Learning

- Dew and frost are sometimes referred to as precipitation. Ask students to explain why dew and frost are not forms of precipitation. *(Dew is a thin film of liquid formed from water vapor that condenses onto the surface of cooled objects near the ground during the nighttime. When the surface temperature of those objects is below 32°F, or 0°C, the water vapor changes directly to solid frost.)*

- Precipitation is part of Earth's water cycle. Have students use a cycle chart to show how the water cycle works.

- Have students design an experiment to show both evaporation and precipitation.

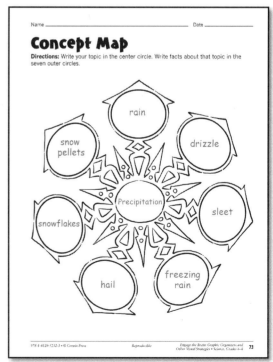

Name _____ Date _____

Concept Map

Directions: Write your topic in the center circle. Write facts about that topic in the seven outer circles.

rain

snow pellets

drizzle

snowflakes

Precipitation

sleet

hail

freezing rain

Precipitation

Precipitation can be any form of rain, snow, or ice. When rising water vapor reaches the upper troposphere, it condenses to form clouds, and the moisture returns to Earth again as precipitation.

Rain: Moisture that falls as drops of liquid.

Drizzle: Fine drops or a mist of water smaller than rain.

Sleet: Frozen raindrops; the rain freezes into small ice pellets as it falls through a cold layer of air, similar to a mixture of rain and snow.

Freezing Rain: The reverse of sleet; rain falls as a liquid but then freezes in a glaze upon contact with the ground, creating dangerous road conditions called "black ice."

Hail: Large pellets of ice that form inside a cumulonimbus cloud; strong updrafts in the cloud carry the pellets up and down through the cold region of the cloud, adding new layers of ice until the pellets are heavy enough to fall to the ground.

Snowflakes: A collection of ice crystals that usually form within high clouds; as the ice crystals move through the air, they sweep up water vapor and grow.

Snow Pellets: Also known as "soft hail"; they develop when snowflakes partially melt and then refreeze, giving them the characteristics of hail, sleet, and snow.

Name _____ Date _____

Concept Map

Directions: Write your topic in the center circle. Write facts about that topic in the seven outer circles.

Rivers of the World: Bar Graph

Materials

Rivers of the World reproducible

research materials about geography (rivers)

colored pencils or markers

chart paper

rulers

overhead projector and transparency

Skills Objectives

Represent and interpret data in a bar graph.

Recognize patterns.

Bar graphs are simple visual models that allow students to present information clearly and interpret data at a glance. They may be used to show quantity or frequency. They are also an appealing way to illustrate trends, compare facts and statistics, and show results of surveys.

1. Write these activities on the board: *riverboat ride, whitewater rafting, canoeing, kayaking, fishing.* Take a survey, asking students to vote for their favorite activity. Record the results on the board. Then explain that a more visual and effective way to show and compare the results is to draw a bar graph.

2. Illustrate how to make a simple vertical bar graph of the results on chart paper. Write a number scale from 1 to 10 along the vertical axis (*y*-axis) and the activity names along the horizontal axis (*x*-axis). Draw different colored bars to show the number of votes for each activity. Invite volunteers to help you label and draw each part of the bar graph. After the graph is complete, have students compare and interpret the results. Ask questions such as: *Which activity was chosen the most? Which was chosen the least? Why do you think so?*

3. Tell students that a survey is only one way a bar graph may be used to relay information. Give them a copy of the **Rivers of the World reproducible (page 76)**, and place a transparency of the reproducible on the overhead.

4. Explain that a bar graph can also be used to compare sizes, such as lengths of rivers. Tell students they will research the lengths and locations of the world's ten longest rivers and then make a bar graph of those lengths. Lengths should be rounded to the nearest hundred before graphing. Ask students: *Why do you think it's a good idea to use rounded values instead of exact values?* (It's difficult to accurately graph

small amounts when dealing with a range in the thousands; reported sizes of rivers may vary in different resources, so using rounded values will eliminate that discrepancy.)

5. Demonstrate how to start filling in the Rivers of the World reproducible using the lengths of the Nile River (4,160 miles) and the Amazon River (4,000 miles). With students, decide on a possible number scale, bar graph orientation, and labels. After demonstrating how to draw the first two bars, point out that it might be better to complete the data chart first to make sure the number scale is appropriate for all the values. Remind students that the increments of a number scale must stay consistent.

6. Provide students with research materials to complete the data chart and bar graph. Encourage partners to compare data before making their graph. If their values don't match, have them check another source and/or calculate the average.

7. Monitor students as they work, making sure they understand how to set up and draw their graphs. Encourage them to use a ruler and different colored pencils or markers to draw the bars. Remind them to space the bars equally, draw them with the same width, double-check the heights for accuracy, and include all labels.

8. After students complete their graphs, discuss the results. Ask questions such as: *What are the ten longest rivers in the world?* (Nile, Amazon, Yangtze, Huang He, Ob-Irtysh, Amur, Lena, Congo, Mackenzie, Mekong) *Which river is the longest?* (Nile) *How many of the rivers are less than 3,000 miles long?* (five) Encourage students to ask their own questions.

9. Display the completed results on a bulletin board, and encourage students to add information cards and drawings to complete the display.

Extended Learning

Ask students to bring in examples of bar graphs and other kind of graphs from magazines and newspapers to compare and discuss.

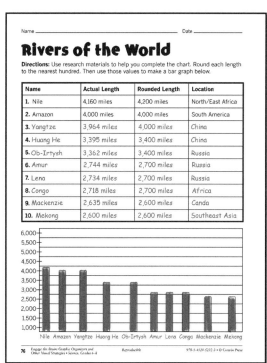

Name _____ Date _____

Rivers of the World

Directions: Use research materials to help you complete the chart. Round each length to the nearest hundred. Then use those values to make a bar graph below.

Name	Actual Length	Rounded Length	Location
1. Nile	4,160 miles	4,200 miles	North/East Africa
2. Amazon	4,000 miles	4,000 miles	South America
3. Yangtze	3,964 miles	4,000 miles	China
4. Huang He	3,395 miles	3,400 miles	China
5. Ob-Irtysh	3,362 miles	3,400 miles	Russia
6. Amur	2,744 miles	2,700 miles	Russia
7. Lena	2,734 miles	2,700 miles	Russia
8. Congo	2,718 miles	2,700 miles	Africa
9. Mackenzie	2,635 miles	2,600 miles	Canda
10. Mekong	2,600 miles	2,600 miles	Southeast Asia

Name _____ Date _____

Rivers of the World

Directions: Use research materials to help you complete the chart. Round each length to the nearest hundred. Then use those values to make a bar graph below.

Name	Actual Length	Rounded Length	Location
1. Nile	4,160 miles	4,200 miles	North/East Africa
2. Amazon	4,000 miles	4,000 miles	South America
3.			
4.			
5.			
6.			
7.			
8.			
9.			
10.			

 Engage the Brain: Graphic Organizers and Other Visual Strategies • Science, Grades 6–8   *Reproducible*   978-1-4129-5232-3 • © *Corwin Press*

Forces of Nature: Cause and Effect Map

Skills Objectives

Recognize cause-and-effect relationships.
Predict results.

Identifying cause-and-effect relationships encourages students to think critically and recognize a likely outcome. **Cause and Effect Maps** illustrate how actions are linked to predictable results.

1. Write the words *Cause* and *Effect* on the board, and write *rain* below the word *Cause.* Ask the class: *What might happen if it began to pour rain in the middle of recess?* (Everyone would get wet. Everyone would go indoors.) List students' responses on the board below the word *Effect,* pointing out the cause-and-effect relationship. Ask students to suggest other cause-and-effect relationships, and record their ideas. Point out that one cause can lead to more than one effect or a chain of causes and effects.

2. Give students a copy of the **Volcanoes** and **Cause and Effect Map reproducibles (pages 79–80)**. Place a transparency of the Cause and Effect Map on the overhead projector. Tell the class they will be working together to list causes and effects mentioned in the "Volcanoes" article. Ask a volunteer to read the article aloud as the rest of the class listens.

3. Work with students to fill out the Cause and Effect Map about volcanoes. Begin by asking: *What is the first step that leads to a volcanic eruption?* (magma accumulates underground) *What is the effect of that magma?* (gas bubbles) Go through the process step by step, identifying the causes and effects and listing them on the map. Have students do the same on their map.

4. Point out the chain reaction, noting that each effect in turn becomes the cause of another effect in the series: *Magma accumulates underground → Gas bubbles form → Pressure builds → The volcano erupts → Lava and mud flow → Forests are destroyed → Habitats are affected.*

Materials

Volcanoes reproducible

Cause and Effect Map reproducible

research materials about forces of nature (earthquakes, floods, hurricanes, tornadoes, avalanches)

colored pencils or markers

overhead projector and transparency

5. Give students another copy of the Cause and Effect Map reproducible. Have them research and write about another force of nature, such as an earthquake, flood, hurricane, tornado, or avalanche. Tell them to use their map to list and describe a chain reaction of causes and effects that lead to a final outcome. Encourage students to include illustrations or pictures of each step in the process.

6. Ask volunteers to read their completed maps to the class. Have classmates predict each effect before it is read aloud, and encourage them to suggest more causes and effects for each situation.

Extended Learning

- Ask students to examine their completed cause and effect maps and predict how the outcome would change if one of the causes changed. Invite them to complete a new map based on this change.

- Have students bring in newspaper articles that show cause and effect. As a class, identify each cause and effect in the articles.

- Tell students to think of an important event in their life and create a cause and effect map of this event.

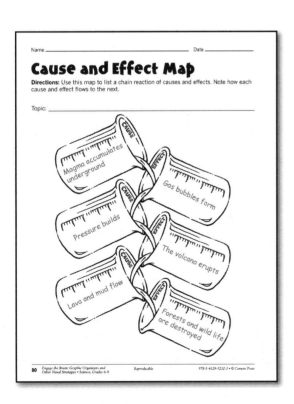

Volcanoes

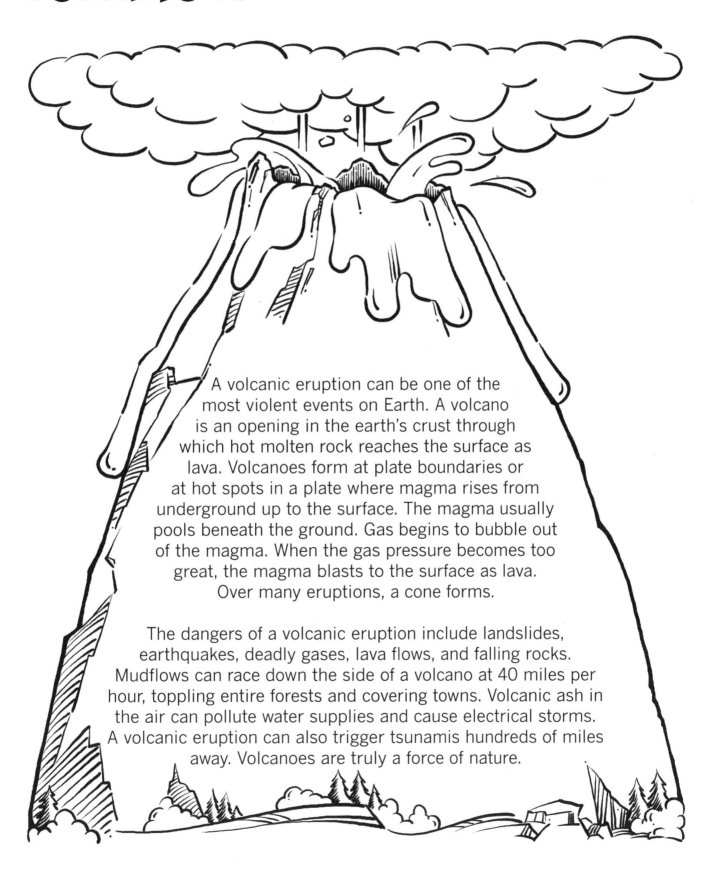

A volcanic eruption can be one of the most violent events on Earth. A volcano is an opening in the earth's crust through which hot molten rock reaches the surface as lava. Volcanoes form at plate boundaries or at hot spots in a plate where magma rises from underground up to the surface. The magma usually pools beneath the ground. Gas begins to bubble out of the magma. When the gas pressure becomes too great, the magma blasts to the surface as lava. Over many eruptions, a cone forms.

The dangers of a volcanic eruption include landslides, earthquakes, deadly gases, lava flows, and falling rocks. Mudflows can race down the side of a volcano at 40 miles per hour, toppling entire forests and covering towns. Volcanic ash in the air can pollute water supplies and cause electrical storms. A volcanic eruption can also trigger tsunamis hundreds of miles away. Volcanoes are truly a force of nature.

Cause and Effect Map

Directions: Use this map to list a chain reaction of causes and effects. Note how each cause and effect flows to the next.

Topic: _____

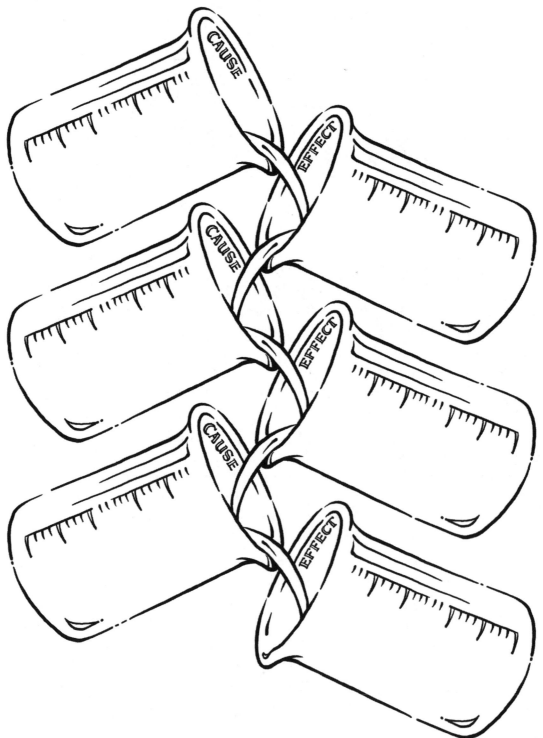

978-1-4129-5232-3 • © Corwin Press

Earth's Crust: Pie Graph

Skills Objectives
Use percents to express data.
Compare parts to a whole.

Materials
Earth's Crust
reproducible

calculators

protractors

colored pencils or
markers

A **Pie Graph** helps students to present a visual overview of information. It is an excellent graph for expressing a set of data in a report or on a poster. Divided into sections that represent percentages or fractions, the pie graph allows students to quickly compare different parts of the same whole.

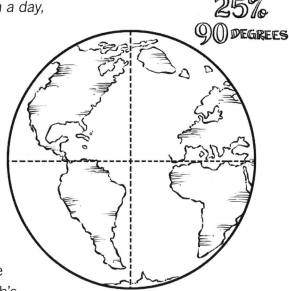

25%
90 DEGREES

1. Ask students how many hours of sleep they should get each night. *(about eight hours)* Ask: *There are 24 hours in a day, so about what percentage is for sleep?* (about 30%) Draw a circle on the board, and label it *Pie Graph*. Explain that a pie graph shows parts of a whole using fractions or percents totaling one whole or 100%. Divide the circle into three equal sections, and label one *Sleep 30%*. Then work with students to complete the rest of the graph using *Daytime Hours in School* and *Daytime Hours Outside of School*.

2. Ask students to suggest other information that could be shown on a pie graph. Encourage them to think of scientific data. Then give them a copy of the **Earth's Crust reproducible (page 83)**. Explain that the earth's crust is comprised of many elements, mostly oxygen, silicon, aluminum, and iron.

3. Draw another circle on the board and label it *Earth's Crust*. Work with students to complete the chart of Earth's elements as shown below. Explain: *To determine the portion of the circle to use for each element in our pie graph, we need to change the percent to a decimal and then multiply by 360° (the degrees of a whole circle). For example, 47% or 0.47 x 360° = 169.2° or 170° rounded to the nearest ten, which is almost half the circle.*

Element	Percent	Decimal	Degrees of a Circle	Rounded
Oxygen	47%	0.47	x 360° = 169.2°	170°
Silicon	28%	0.28	x 360° = 100.8°	100°
Aluminum	8%	0.08	x 360° = 28.8°	30°
Iron	5%	0.05	x 360° = 18.0°	20°
Others	12%	0.12	x 360° = 43.2°	40°

4. Model how to use a protractor to draw each section of the pie graph using the rounded values. Or, have students use a pencil and straightedge to lightly divide the circle into 12 equal sections (30 degrees per section) and estimate the number of sections to fill for each element (*Oxygen*, a little less than six sections; *Silicon*, a little more than three sections; *Aluminum*, one section; *Iron*, a little less than one section; *Others*, a little more than one section). Write the name and percentage in each section.

5. After creating part of the pie graph with students and checking for understanding, have students finish it on their own and color the sections. Monitor their progress.

6. Display and discuss the completed graphs. Ask students if they thought the pie graphs were the best way to show the data or if another type of graph would have worked as well. Invite them to share their ideas.

Extended Learning

- Have students make another pie graph showing more of Earth's elements by dividing the *Others* section: oxygen 47%, silicon 28%, aluminum 8%, iron 5%, calcium 4%, sodium 3%, potassium 3%, magnesium 2%.

- For additional practice with pie graphs, draw samples with missing sections, and ask students to determine the percent of each missing part.

- Suggest that students use computer graphics or go online and use the Interactive Circle Graph maker at: *www.shodor.org/interactivate/activities/circlegraph.*

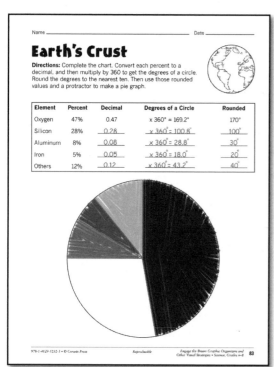

Name _____ Date _____

Earth's Crust

Directions: Complete the chart. Convert each percent to a decimal, and then multiply by 360 to get the degrees of a circle. Round the degrees to the nearest ten. Then use those rounded values and a protractor to make a pie graph.

Element	Percent	Decimal	Degrees of a Circle	Rounded
Oxygen	47%	0.47	x 360° = 169.2°	170°
Silicon	28%	0.28	x 360° = 100.8°	100°
Aluminum	8%	0.08	x 360° = 28.8°	30°
Iron	5%	0.05	x 360° = 18.0°	20°
Others	12%	0.12	x 360° = 43.2°	40°

Earth's Crust

Directions: Complete the chart. Convert each percent to a decimal, and then multiply by 360 to get the degrees of a circle. Round the degrees to the nearest ten. Then use those rounded values and a protractor to make a pie graph.

Element	Percent	Decimal	Degrees of a Circle	Rounded
Oxygen	47%	0.47	x 360° = 169.2°	170°
Silicon	28%	_____	_____	_____
Aluminum	8%	_____	_____	_____
Iron	5%	_____	_____	_____
Others	12%	_____	_____	_____

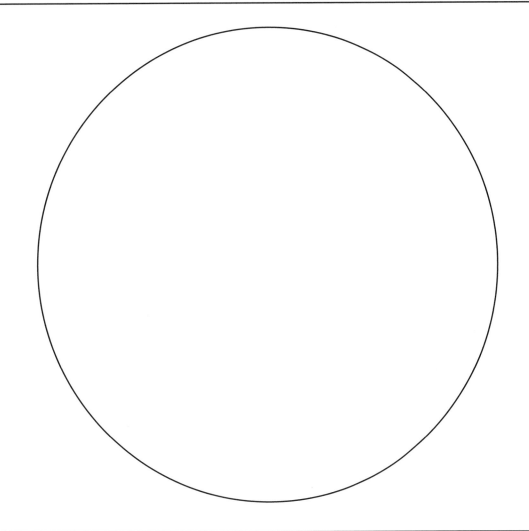

Earth Eras: Timeline

Materials

Earth Eras Timeline reproducible

research materials about Earth's history

white construction paper

rulers

scissors

glue

colored pencils or markers

Skills Objectives

Identify relevant details and key information.

Visualize key moments in chronological order.

A **Timeline** is a straightforward means of allowing students to order events in chronological sequence. It may be used to show a short-term sequence over the course of a season or year or a long-term sequence over millions of years.

1. Ask students what their lives would be like if they lived in the last Ice Age. Have them consider how they would spend their time and how they would get food, protect themselves, clean, and sleep. For example, to bathe, students might use water warmed from a fire. They could brush their teeth with a small twig and eat mammoth meat for dinner. They could spend the day hunting, preparing food, and making tools and clothing; and at night, they might sleep on a bed of fur.

2. Have students discuss some of the advances and inventions humans have made since then, from the use of certain metals to the development of cars and computers. Explain that such progression can be shown in chronological order on a timeline. Ask a volunteer to define *chronological order* (putting events in order from the earliest to the most recent event) and describe a *timeline* (a graphic display of chronological events). Tell students they will be making a timeline about Earth.

3. Give each student a sheet of construction paper, a ruler, scissors, glue, and a copy of the **Earth Eras Timeline reproducible (page 86)**. Draw a long horizontal line on the board, and demonstrate how to set up the timeline from left to right in chronological order, writing the dates above the line and the corresponding events below the line. For example, ask students to tell you which date on their reproducible is the earliest. Write *4.5 billion years ago* above the line at the beginning of the timeline. Then ask students which event belongs with that date. Write *Earth forms* below the line. Write several dates and events with students, checking for understanding.

4. Instruct students to use a ruler to draw a straight line across the middle of their construction paper and then use the cutouts from their reproducible to create a timeline of life on Earth. Tell them to cut apart the labels from the reproducible and match up the events and dates in chronological order before gluing anything to their timeline. Monitor their progress as they work, offering assistance as needed.

5. Encourage students to check their work with a partner. Ask them what observations can be made about Earth's history based on their timeline. For example: *Which came first, mammals or reptiles? What does the timeline show about the development of human beings?*

6. Encourage students to expand their timelines, adding factual information about each era and extending their timeline to include more recent events. Provide students with research materials about Earth's history. Encourage them to draw symbols and/or illustrations for each event.

7. Display the completed timelines, and ask students to identify the similarities and differences. Emphasize the usefulness of using a timeline to study science.

Extended Learning

- Have students create a timeline of their own lives. Encourage them to include pictures and descriptions.

- During Earth's history there have been at least five mass extinctions. Have students research information about those extinctions and create a timeline. Ask how such extinctions may have affected the development of life on Earth.

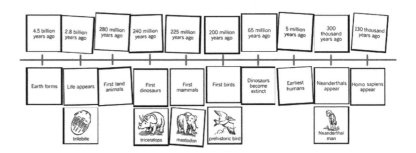

Name _____ Date _____

Earth Eras Timeline

Directions: Cut apart and organize the labels and pictures to create a timeline about Earth. Draw a long line on a large sheet of paper. In chronological order, glue each date above the line and the corresponding event below the line. Then glue the pictures below the time period during which the living thing first appeared.

Earth forms	Life appears	First land animals	First dinosaurs	First mammals
First birds	Dinosaurs become extinct	Earliest humans	Neanderthals appear	Homo sapiens appear
4.5 billion years ago	2.8 billion years ago	280 million years ago	240 million years ago	225 million years ago
200 million years ago	65 million years ago	5 million years ago	300 thousand years ago	130 thousand years ago
trilobite	triceratops	mastodon	prehistoric bird	Neanderthal man

 Engage the Brain: Graphic Organizers and Other Visual Strategies • Science, Grades 6–8   *Reproducible*   978-1-4129-5232-3 • © Corwin Press

Tectonics: Puzzle and Jigsaw Map

Skills Objectives
Sort out relationships in complex ideas or events.
Understand motions and forces.

Materials
Jigsaw Map reproducible

world map or globe

9" x 12" cardstock or poster board

colored pencils or markers

glue sticks

scissors

resealable plastic bags

Most students enjoy **Puzzles**. A simple jigsaw puzzle can be used to introduce new concepts in a fun and interesting way. Puzzles are a good tool for reinforcing learning, particularly when it comes to visual information such as maps, charts, and diagrams.

1. Have students close their eyes and sit quietly for a moment. Explain that although they may not be feeling it, the earth below them is moving. The earth's crust is made up of large plates of moving rock that inch across the surface of the planet. The plates are continuously separating, bumping into each other, and sliding past or over each other. This constant motion is called *plate tectonics* and is responsible in part for shaping the earth as we know it.

2. Display a world map or globe to the class. Explain that the earth's crust is like a jigsaw puzzle of land pieces. Ask students: *Which land masses do you think could fit together like pieces of a jigsaw puzzle? Look at the coastlines of Africa and South America. How do you think they could fit together?* Point out that each of the continents is associated with a major tectonic plate.

3. Give each student a sheet of cardstock, colored pencils or markers, scissors, a glue stick, a resealable plastic bag, and a copy of the **Jigsaw Map reproducible (page 89)**.

4. Ask students to color in the continents and then glue the entire map onto cardstock for durability. Point out the borders of the tectonic plates on the reproducible, and instruct students to cut along those lines that form the borders. (Note that the borders are usually deep underwater.) Monitor students as they work, and make sure they are cutting out the tectonic plates and not the continents.

5. When they are finished, have students mix up their cutouts and put them back together again like a jigsaw puzzle. After they put together their puzzle, they can store their puzzle pieces in a resealable plastic bag.

6. Invite students to share how this experience helped them better understand the concept of plate tectonics. Have them go online or use other resources to compare their tectonic plates puzzle to *Pangaea* (the supercontinent believed to have existed about 250 million years ago, before the process of plate tectonics separated the continents and other land masses into their current configuration).

Extended Learning

• Encourage students to create other types of puzzles based on information about plate tectonics, such as word finds, crossword puzzles, word searches, and word jumbles. Invite students to solve each other's puzzles.

• Divide the class into five groups, and assign each group one of the following topics to research and present to the class: plate tectonics and earthquakes; plate tectonics and volcanoes; how the plates move, fueled by Earth's internal heat; plate tectonics, mid-ocean ridges; plate tectonics and the ring of fire.

• Have students go to the Windows to the Universe Web site to see how plate tectonics have changed Earth's surface over time: *www.windows.ucar.edu/tour/link=/earth/past/geologic_time.html.*

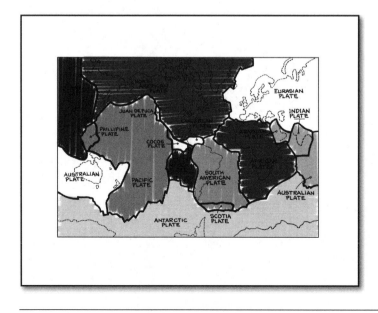

Jigsaw Map

Directions: Color the map and glue it onto cardstock. Then cut apart the map along the tectonic plate boundaries to create a jigsaw puzzle of Earth's surface.

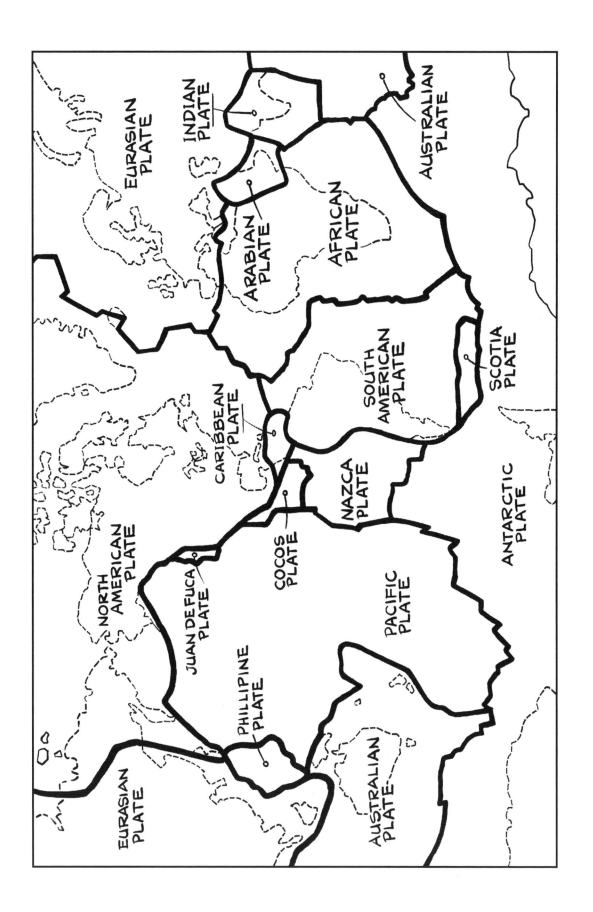

Our Solar System: KWL Chart

<table>
<tr><td>

Materials

KWL Chart reproducible

research materials about the solar system

</td><td>

Skills Objectives

Read for a purpose.
Use prior knowledge.
Identify relevant details and key information.

</td></tr>
</table>

Students are naturally curious about the world and their place in it. Acquiring knowledge about a topic usually leads to further questions. The **KWL Chart** prepares students by having them tap into previous knowledge, anticipate what will come next, develop questions, target information, and summarize what they learn. The chart can also be used as a study guide or a source for a report outline.

1. Begin by having a class discussion about Earth's place in the solar system. Write *Earth* in the center of a big circle on the board, and write *Universe* on the outside of the circle. Ask students to name Earth's neighbors as you write their names inside the circle. Prompt students to name the other planets, the moon, the sun, and smaller objects such as asteroids and comets.

2. Give students a copy of the **KWL Chart reproducible (page 92)**, and draw a copy on the board. Write *Earth and the Solar System* as the topic. Explain that the **K** stands for what students already *know*, the **W** stands for what they *want to know*, and the **L** stands for what they *learn*.

3. Have students look back at the names written on the board, and ask them to share what they know about each of those celestial objects. Record their responses in the *K* column of your KWL chart. Have students do the same on their own chart. Answers might include: *There are eight planets in our solar system. The largest planet is Jupiter. Mercury is closest to the sun.*

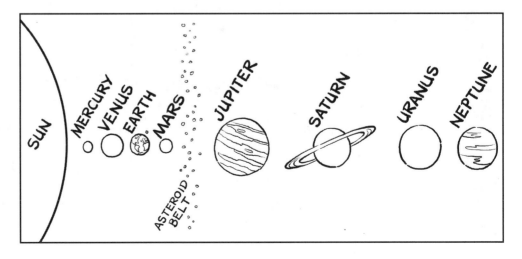

4. Next, have students share what they want to know about Earth and the solar system, such as: *How far is Earth from the sun? How long will the sun last? Why is Pluto no longer considered a planet?* Write their responses in the *W* column of your KWL chart while students do the same on their own chart.

5. Encourage students to add more information to their chart, writing other facts they know or would like to know about the solar system. Suggest that they consider both past and present events, people involved with space exploration, and how Earth relates to other celestial bodies in space.

6. Have students work independently or with a partner to research facts about the solar system. Provide nonfiction books, magazines, encyclopedias, Internet access, and other reference materials. Tell students to record what they learn in the *L* column of their KWL Chart.

7. Once the activity is complete, ask students how their KWL Chart helped with their research. Invite them to share and compare their answers from the *L* column of their charts.

Extended Learning

- Divide the class into eight groups and assign each group a planet. Have each group create a travel brochure to convince space travelers to visit their assigned planet. Provide sample travel brochures for students to review. Encourage them to use computer technology to design and create their brochures.

- Discuss some of the misconceptions people have had about the solar system over the centuries, why people might have thought those things, and the reality behind the myths. For example: *Mars has canals with flowing water. Saturn is the only planet with rings. Venus is covered with oceans.* Encourage students to create a "fact or fiction" game about the solar system.

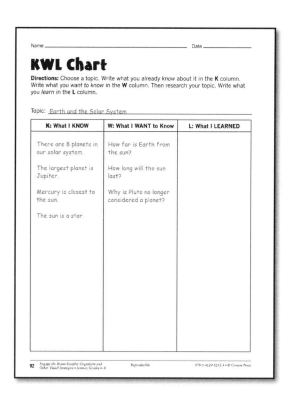

KWL Chart

Directions: Choose a topic. Write what you already *know* about it in the **K** column. Write what you *want to know* in the **W** column. Then research your topic. Write what you *learn* in the **L** column.

Topic: _____

K: What I KNOW	W: What I WANT to Know	L: What I LEARNED

Advances in Science: 5W Chart

Skills Objectives

Conduct scientific inquiry.

Read for a purpose.

Record facts accurately.

Organize and communicate information.

Materials

5W Chart reproducible

newspaper articles that focus on science

highlighters

The newspaper has always been an important tool in the classroom. It generally offers a concise, tightly organized story with clearly stated facts. Using a **5W Chart** in conjunction with a newspaper encourages students to focus carefully on important facts and details. A 5W chart also helps students sort out the **W**ho, **W**hen, **W**here, **W**hat, and **W**hy of a newspaper article or other form of nonfiction.

1. Ask students to bring in newspaper articles about space exploration and other scientific topics, or bring in newspapers from which students can choose articles.

2. Explain that for newspaper articles and other kinds of nonfiction, students must answer five questions in order to get all the facts. These questions are known as the five W's—*who, what, when, where,* and *why*. Write those words on the board, and demonstrate how to sort facts into these categories using a current event, such as a recent school event or celebrity news. Point out that the five W's summarize the event.

3. Give students a copy of the **5W Chart reproducible (page 95)**. Tell them to read a newspaper article about a scientific topic and answer the five W's on their chart—*who* the article is about or *who* made a discovery, *what* happened, *when* it happened, *where* it happened, and *why* it happened. Have students use a highlighter to mark important facts in the article.

4. When students are finished, discuss whether or not they thought their articles were newsworthy. Ask: *Was your article informative? Why or why not? What other questions about this story would you like to have answered? Did you find all answers to the five W's?*

5. Have students use what they have learned and do some additional research to write their own article about a recent advance in science. They can use another 5W chart to organize and record their facts. Encourage students to include a captivating title and detailed pictures or diagrams.

6. Invite volunteers to read their articles to the class. Have classmates take notes while they listen and identify *who, what, when, where,* and *why.*

Extended Learning

- Have students write a one- or two-sentence summary about the article they read and draw a picture to accompany it.

- Encourage students to use computer technology to write their articles in a newspaper layout, including a headline and pictures with captions.

- Introduce students to science magazines such as *Astronomy* and *Sky and Telescope*. Have students read one or two articles, and then discuss how newspaper articles and magazine articles are alike and different. You might also print out articles from the following science Web sites:

    www.nasa.gov

    www.sciencemag.org

    www.discovermagazine.com

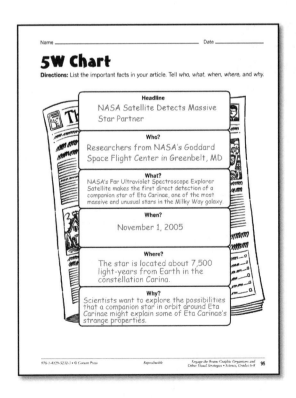

5W Chart

Directions: List the important facts in your article. Tell *who, what, when, where,* and *why.*

Headline

Who?

What?

When?

Where?

Why?

References

Australian Museum Online. (2004). *Metamorphosis: A remarkable change.* Retrieved October 20, 2006, from www.amonline.net.au/insects/insects/metamorphosis.htm.

Baker, D. (1982). *The history of manned space flight* (pp. 17–29). New York, NY: New Cavendish Books.

Bromley, K., Irwin-De Vitis, L., & Modlo, M. (1995). *Graphic organizers: Visual strategies for active learning.* New York, NY: Scholastic Professional Books.

Byers, J. (2004). *Instructional strategies online: What are graphic organizers?* Retrieved August 15, 2006, from the Saskatoon Public School Division, Inc., Online Learning Center Web site: http://olc.spsd.sk.ca/DE/PD/instr/strats/graphicorganizers.

Chem1 Virtual Textbook. (2006). *Classification and properties of matter.* Retrieved October 10, 2006, from http://www.chem1.com/adad/webtext/pre/matter.html.

Couper, H., & Henbest, N. (1992). *The space atlas* (pp. 14–17). London, England: Dorling Kindersley.

Deutsch, G., & Neal-Jones, N. (2005). *NASA satellite detects massive star partner.* Retrieved October 12, 2006, from the NASA Web site: http://www.nasa.gov/home/hqnews/2005/nov/HQ_05353_massive_star.html.

Forte, I., & Schurr, S. (2001). *Standards-based language arts graphic organizers, rubrics, and writing prompts for middle grade students.* Nashville, TN: Incentive Publications, Inc.

Gardner, H. (1983). *Frames of mind: The theory of multiple intelligences.* New York, NY: Basic Books.

Graphic.org. (n.d.). *Graphic organizers.* Retrieved August 10, 2006, from http://www.graphic.org.

Hall, T., & Strangman, N. (2002). *Graphic organizers.* Wakefield, MA: National Center on Accessing the General Curriculum. Retrieved August 15, 2006, from the CAST: Universal Design for Learning Web site: http://www.cast.org/publications/ncac/ncac_go.html.

Hopkins, G. (2003). *Strategy of the week: Debates in the classroom.* Retrieved September 20, 2006, from the Education World Web site: http://www.education/world.com/a_curr/strategy/strategy012.shtml.

Jensen, E., & Johnson, G. (1994). *The learning brain.* San Diego, CA: Turning Point for Teachers.

McCarthy, B. (1990). Using the 4MAT system to bring learning styles to schools. *Educational Leadership, 48*(2), 31–37.

Mohave High School, The Science Classroom. (n.d.). *Graphic organizers.* Retrieved August 10, 2006, from http://gotoscience.com/Graphic_Organizers.html#Toppage.

National Research Council. (2005). *National science education standards.* Washington, DC: National Academy Press.

Novak, J. D., & Cañas, A. J. (2006). *The theory underlying concept maps and how to construct them.* Florida Institute for Human and Machine Cognition (Technical Report IHMC CmapTools 2006-01). Retrieved August 15, 2006, from http://cmap.ihmc.us/Publications/ResearchPapers/TheoryCmaps/TheoryUnderlyingConceptMaps.htm.

Ogle, D. M. (2000). Make it visual: A picture is worth a thousand words. In M. McLaughlin & M. Vogt (Eds.), *Creativity and innovation in content area teaching.* Norwood, MA: Christopher-Gordon.

Robinson, S. M., Haynes, D., Richman, L., & Bode, T. (n.d.). *Instructional planning: Graphic organizers.* Retrieved September 13, 2006, from the University of Kansas, Special Connections Web site: http://www.specialconnections.ku.edu/cgi-bin/cgiwrap/specconn/main.php?cat=instruction&section=main&subsection=udl/graphic.

Simkin, T., Tillig, R. I., Vogt, P. R., Kirby, S. H., Kimberly, P., & Stewart, D. B. (n.d.). *This dynamic planet: World map of volcanoes, earthquakes, impact craters, and plate tectonics.* Retrieved November 5, 2006, from the Smithsonian National Museum of Natural History Web site: http://baird.si.edu/minsci/tdpmap/viewer.htm.

Tate, M. L. (2003). *Worksheets don't grow dendrites: 20 instructional strategies that engage the brain.* Thousand Oaks, CA: Corwin Press.

United States Geological Survey. (2006). *The Water Cycle: Precipitation and Earth's water distribution.* Retrieved November 3, 2006, from http://ga.water.usgs.gov/edu/mearthall.html.